ECONOMIC ISSUES, PROBLEMS AND PERSPECTIVES

INVESTOR BEHAVIOR

PATTERNS AND PITFALLS

ECONOMIC ISSUES, PROBLEMS AND PERSPECTIVES

Additional books in this series can be found on Nova's website under the Series tab.

Additional E-books in this series can be found on Nova's website under the E-books tab.

BUSINESS ISSUES, COMPETITION AND ENTREPRENEURSHIP

Additional books in this series can be found on Nova's website under the Series tab.

Additional E-books in this series can be found on Nova's website under the E-books tab.

ECONOMIC ISSUES, PROBLEMS AND PERSPECTIVES

INVESTOR BEHAVIOR

PATTERNS AND PITFALLS

ANDRE MOLIÉRE
EDITOR

Nova Science Publishers, Inc.
New York

For permission to use material from this book please contact us:
Telephone 631-231-7269; Fax 631-231-8175
Web Site: http://www.novapublishers.com

Library of Congress Cataloging-in-Publication Data

Investor behavior : patterns and pitfalls / editor, Andre Molihre.
p. cm.
Includes bibliographical references and index.
ISBN 978-1-61470-205-4 (softcover)
1. Investments--Psychological aspects. 2. Investments. 3. Investments--Bibliography. I. Moliére, Andre.
HG4515.15.I54 2011
332.601'9--dc23

2011020772

Published by Nova Science Publishers, Inc. † New York

CONTENTS

Preface		**vii**
Chapter 1	Behavioral Patterns and Pitfalls of U.S. Investors *Federal Research Division and Library of Congress*	**1**
Chapter 2	Annotated Bibliography on the Behavioral Characteristics of U.S. Investors *Federal Research Division and Library of Congress*	**23**
Chapter Sources		**71**
Index		**73**

PREFACE

This book examines the behavioral characteristics of U.S. investors wherein the primary goal is to identify common investment mistakes and to provide scholarly commentary from university professors and professionals in the fields of economics, business, finance, psychology and sociology. Insights are provided as to how investors make the initial decision to invest and why some are reluctant to invest at all. Many of the scholars cited here have made seminal contributions to the analysis of the human element of investing. Students of their work can learn much about the patterns and pitfalls associated with investor behavior.

Chapter 1- According to statistical evidence presented in academic studies, patterns of investor behavior are often counterproductive. Drawing on a comprehensive review of academic journal articles, reporting research in the relatively new field of behavioral finance, this paper examines patterns of investor behavior, as well as reasons that individuals are reluctant to invest in the first place. The "Annotated Bibliography on the Behavioral Characteristics of U.S. Investors," also prepared by the Federal Research Division, summarizes the research cited in this paper.

Chapter 2- Investor behavior is a hotly debated topic within the academic community. One relatively new area of study is the field of behavioral finance, which highlights departures from rational behavior in investing. Behavioral finance theory poses a challenge to many of the long-established assumptions of the rational expectations school of thought, which posits that people (investors) maximize utility (returns), acting rationally and in their self-interest. By focusing on the psychological and behavioral elements in the determination of stock prices, behavioral finance also challenges the efficient market hypothesis (EMH), which holds that market prices reflect all known information. EMH, developed by University of Chicago economist and Nobel Laureate Eugene Fama, implies that beating the market by identifying undervalued securities is impossible. Whether EMH remains valid is beyond the scope of this annotated bibliography, which is more concerned with investor behavior than with market efficiency. In other words, how the market behaves is not relevant here. Instead, the focus of this bibliography is on how investors behave and on how investor education may help them avoid common mistakes. This bibliography covers the last 15 years.

In: Investor Behavior: Patterns and Pitfalls ISBN: 978-1-61470-205-4
Editors: Andre Moliére

Chapter 1

BEHAVIORAL PATTERNS AND PITFALLS OF U.S. INVESTORS

Federal Research Division and Library of Congress

OVERVIEW

According to statistical evidence presented in academic studies, patterns of investor behavior are often counterproductive. Drawing on a comprehensive review of academic journal articles, reporting research in the relatively new field of behavioral finance, this paper examines patterns of investor behavior, as well as reasons that individuals are reluctant to invest in the first place. The "Annotated Bibliography on the Behavioral Characteristics of U.S. Investors," also prepared by the Federal Research Division, summarizes the research cited in this paper.

THE ROLE OF BEHAVIORAL FINANCE

Pioneers of the field of behavioral finance set out to challenge the prevailing assumptions of rational expectations theory, which holds that investors act rationally and in their self-interest, aiming to maximize returns at a given level of risk. Behavioral finance adherents emphasize the social, cognitive, or emotional factors that lead investors to depart from the rational behavior that traditional economists assume. As University of California finance professors Brad M. Barber and Terrance Odean explain in their article on "The Courage of Misguided Convictions," behavioral finance incorporates "observable, systematic, and very human departures into standard models of financial markets."[1]

Behavioral finance holds that investors tend to fall into predictable patterns of destructive behavior. In other words, they make the same mistakes repeatedly. Specifically, many investors damage their portfolios by underdiversifying; trading frequently; following the herd; favoring the familiar (domestic stocks, company stock, and glamour stocks); selling winning positions and holding onto losing positions (disposition effect); and succumbing to optimism, short-term thinking, and overconfidence (self-attribution bias).[2]

Prospect Theory

Behavioral finance is a multidisciplinary field that draws on psychology and sociology to shed light on financial behavior. One of the foundations of behavioral finance is prospect theory, developed by Princeton psychology professor Daniel Kahneman, a Nobel Prize laureate, and the late psychologist Amos Tversky, last affiliated with Stanford University. Prospect theory examines how people maximize value or utility in choosing among alternatives that involve risk. As applied to finance, prospect theory posits that, when measuring utility under conditions of uncertainty, investors pay too much attention to incremental gains and losses. Excessive risk aversion leads them to attach more importance to avoiding losses than to achieving gains. As Figure 1 demonstrates in graphical terms, the value function guiding investors is asymmetrical with respect to losses versus gains.

Consequently, investors realize subpar investment returns, rather than maximizing wealth, as rational expectations theory predicts. In an article on "Aspects of Investor Psychology," coauthored with Mark W. Riepe, who specializes in investment products and mutual-fund research at Charles Schwab & Company, Kahneman uses prospect theory to highlight biases of judgment—overconfidence, optimism, hindsight, and overreaction to past events—and errors of preference—assigning probabilities and values to future outcomes. These errors and biases lead to poor investment decisions.[3]

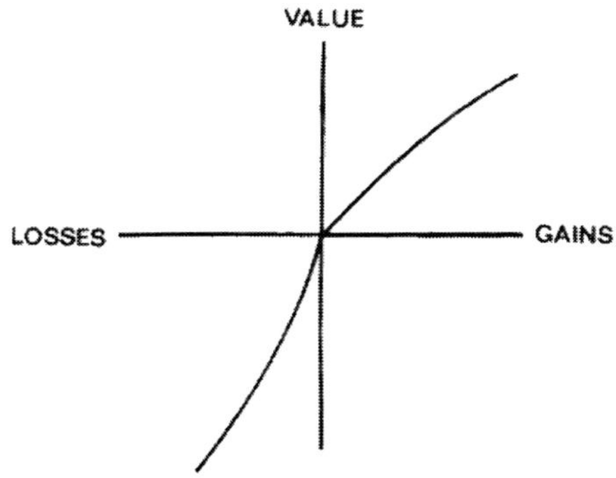

Source: Daniel Kahneman and Amos Tversky, "Prospect Theory: An Analysis of Decision under Risk," *Econometrica* 47, no. 2 (March 1979): 279.

Figure 1. Value Function in Prospect Theory.

Overconfidence

Overconfidence, an emotion common among investors, triggers a wide range of investment errors. In the worst-case outcome, an overconfident investor becomes a victim of some form of investment fraud, such as a Ponzi scheme. In his article, "On Financial Frauds and Their Causes: Investor Overconfidence," Steven Pressman, an economist at Monmouth University, identifies overconfidence as the primary psychological culprit responsible for the susceptibility of otherwise sophisticated investors to financial fraud.[4] Pressman maintains that empirical psychology, which analyzes how people make choices when confronted with uncertainty, offers a better explanation for the success of Ponzi schemes than does neoclassical economics, with its emphasis on the role of asymmetric information in risky situations. Pressman advocates providing the public with more information about the risks of scams, educating potential investors about the details of specific cases of fraud. He also recommends substantially increasing the penalties for such schemes, relative to rewards.

Human Sentiment

Given the role of emotion in investing, some social scientists take a very skeptical view of the stock market in general. In "Money and Sentiment: A

Psychodynamic Approach to Behavioral Finance," medical doctor Ildiko Mohacsy, now deceased, and Heidi Lefer, a member of the professional staff of the CUNY Research Council, describe the stock market as a "conglomeration of human sentiment" (hope, fear, and greed) that is not subject to purely scientific analysis.[5] According to their thesis, investors often engage in wishful or magical thinking rather than logical thinking.

Reluctance to Invest

Many people fail to invest at all or neglect to lay an adequate groundwork for satisfactory retirement income. Financial illiteracy and the lack of trust in financial markets play important roles in curbing participation in retirement plans. Therefore, employer-sponsored retirement plans that require opt-in participation often encounter inertia and passivity on the part of employees.

In "Lessons from Behavioral Finance for Retirement Plan Design," Olivia S. Mitchell of the University of Pennsylvania and Stephen P. Utkus of the Vanguard Group summarize the key findings of behavioral finance regarding pension design and structure.[6] First, the article examines the fundamental issue of how people make their initial economic decision to save for retirement. Moving beyond conventional wisdom on the rational allocation of resources over a lifetime, the authors discuss how and why individuals who choose to save make flawed decisions, dependent on the extent of their self-control and on their limited information, time, and cognitive ability ("bounded rationality"). Mitchell and Utkus suggest that choices regarding whether or not to save reflect an individual's subjective discount rate, applied to the time value of money. They designate those individuals who tend to defer consumption in order to save as "exponential discounters," calling those who save little or nothing "hyperbolic discounters." A s shown in Figure 2, exponential discounters assign a higher value to future money than hyperbolic discounters do.

Behavioral finance theorists also note that conventional economic theory cannot explain the extent to which the design of a retirement plan affects investment decisions. Retirement plans featuring automatic enrollment have much higher participation rates than those in which enrollment is discretionary, because individuals tend to acquiesce in participating and to accept the plan's default options. Furthermore, when a retirement plan's provisions require participants to sign up for (opt into) a retirement plan, individuals tend to procrastinate or to do nothing.

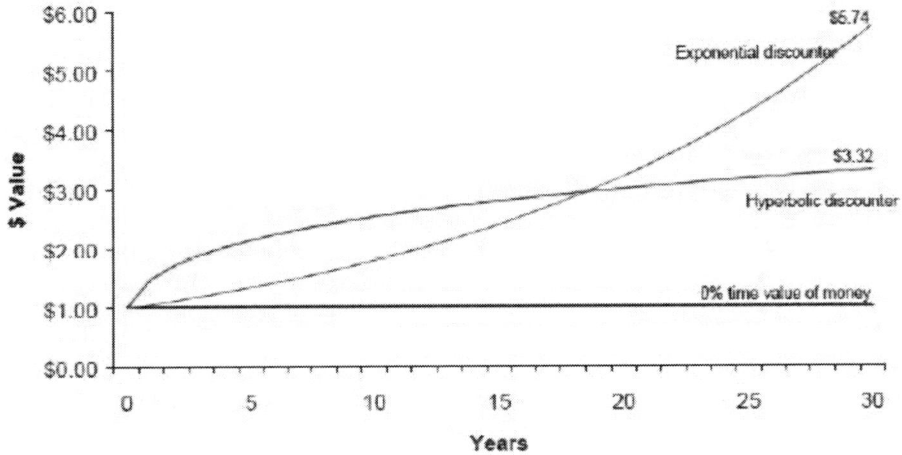

Source: Olivia S. Mitchell and Stephen P. Utkus, "Lessons from Behavioral Finance for Retirement Plan Design," in *Pension Design and Structure: New Lessons from Behavioral Finance*, ed. Mitchell and Utkus, 3–41 (Oxford: Oxord University Press, 2004), 7.

Figure 2. Hyperbolic vs. Exponential Discounting.

Lack of Financial Literacy

Reluctance to invest in the stock market is often the result of financial illiteracy. In "Financial Literacy and Stock Market Participation," Maarten van Rooij, affiliated with the Dutch Central Bank, Rob Alessie of Utrecht University, and Annamaria Lusardi of Dartmouth College use data from the Netherlands to show that people with low financial literacy are less likely to invest in stocks than those who are financially literate.[7] In fact, financial illiteracy not only correlates with the choice not to invest, but causes it. While most households know about basic financial concepts, such as compound interest, inflation, and the time value of money, very few households understand the more advanced financial concepts often considered necessary for successful investing, such as the difference between stocks and bonds, the inverse relationship of bond prices and interest rates, and risk diversification.

In "Financial Literacy and Planning: Implications for Retirement Wellbeing," Lusardi and Mitchell report widespread financial illiteracy among Americans, particularly among women, minorities, and those without a college degree.[8] Furthermore, the authors find a link between financial literacy and retirement planning. Moreover, financially literate investors who plan for the future tend to use formal tools and methods rather than relying on relatives and coworkers for advice. Since investment success is dependent on planning, wide disparities in household wealth upon retirement, between those who plan and those who do not, are no surprise. The study reveals that, overall, only a minority of households feel confident about the adequacy of their retirement saving. The authors recommend financial education programs targeting the least financially sophisticated segments of the population.

Lack of Trust

Lack of trust is another explanation for the reluctance to invest. In "Trusting the Stock Market," the authors—Luigi Guiso of the European University Institute, Paola Sapienza of Northwestern University, and Luigi Zingales of the University of Chicago—attribute limited participation in the stock market, particularly among wealthy investors, to a lack of trust and to the fear of being cheated by participants in the capital markets.[9] Subjective and cultural factors determine how trusting people are, as well as whether and how much they are willing to invest.

Retirement Saving Inadequacy

Jonathan Skinner, an economics professor at Dartmouth College, uses the life-cycle model to examine the question of whether people are saving enough for retirement, reporting his findings in the article, "Are You Sure You're Saving Enough for Retirement?"[10] The life-cycle model assumes that a person tries to maintain a relatively stable ("smooth") standard of living over the course of his or her lifetime, and that this pattern continues through retirement, when that person draws on savings accumulated during his or her career. Skinner attempts to determine how much nonhousing net worth retired people require to continue smooth consumption. His findings indicate that those who save at high rates during their working lives are accustomed to consuming less and, therefore, do not need as much for retirement. Because they have set aside more, this pattern of saving more and consuming less provides investors with a double dividend. They benefit twice: first from becoming accustomed to a modest standard of living and second from saving more. Therefore, the author recommends saving incrementally more each year. Even if most American households fall short of the targets that the life-cycle model stipulates, they may have lower expenses during retirement—except for health care expenses—and may find that they are able to compensate for inadequate savings by economizing. However, Skinner identifies growing out-of-pocket health-care costs as a cause for concern.

COMMON INVESTMENT MISTAKES

Researchers have identified a number of common investment mistakes and have scrutinized some significant patterns of negative investment behavior. Counterproductive patterns targeted in the literature include active trading, the disposition effect, paying more attention to the past performance of mutual funds than to fees, familiarity bias, mania and panic, momentum investing, naïve diversification, noise trading, and underdiversification.

Active Trading

In "Trading is Hazardous to Your Wealth: The Common Stock Investment Performance of Individual Investors," Brad M. Barber and Terrance Odean demonstrate the pitfalls of active trading.[11] According to their study, active traders underperform the market. Active trading correlates with overconfidence. For example, in "Boys Will Be Boys: Gender, Over-confidence, and Common Stock Investment," Barber and Odean find a correlation between male overconfidence and excessive trading, particularly when comparing single men and single women. [12] Because women are less likely to indulge in excessive trading, they outperform men. In "Online Investors: Do the Slow Die First?" Barber and Odean determine that investors who use traditional brokers, remaining in touch with them by telephone, achieve better results than online traders, who damage their performance by trading more actively and speculatively.[13]

Disposition Effect

The disposition effect is the tendency of investors to sell winning positions and to hold onto losing positions. In his study of this effect, Terrance Odean poses the question: "Are Investors Reluctant to Realize Their

Losses?"[14] He answers in the affirmative, demonstrating that the disposition effect is widely operative and that this investment strategy is counterproductive. According to Odean's study, in the months following the sale of winning investments, these investments continue to outperform the losing ones still held in the investment portfolio, an outcome exactly the opposite of that intended. Loss-averse investors sell high- performing investments hoping to recoup their losses on poor performers but, in fact, achieve the reverse. In "Myopic Loss Aversion and the Equity Risk Premium," Shlomo Benartzi and Richard H. Thaler, business school professors at the University of California Los Angeles and the University of Chicago, respectively, coin the term "myopic loss aversion" to describe the tendency of loss-averse investors—even if long-term investors—to evaluate their portfolios frequently.[15] The authors consider the long-term investors' focus on short-term results an unfortunate form of myopia applied to investing.

Paying More Attention to the Past Returns of Mutual Funds than to Fees

In "On Persistence in Mutual Fund Performance," Mark M. Carhart, former professor of finance at the University of Southern California, concludes that expense ratios, transaction costs, and load fees—costs that investors tend to disregard—all harm mutual-fund returns.[16] Such fees are associated with actively managed funds, in which the portfolio manager has discretion over purchases, in contrast to index funds, which mirror a benchmark index. Despite the popularity of actively managed funds, Carhart sees no evidence that portfolio managers are particularly skilled or informed, characteristics that would justify additional fees. Nevertheless, a key finding of another study indicates that full disclosure of these active management fees does not deter investors from selecting this type of fund. In their article, "Why Does the Law of One Price Fail? An Experiment on Index Mutual Funds," by James J. Choi, of Yale School of Management, David Laibson of Harvard's Department of Economics, and Brigitte C. Madrian, of Harvard's Kennedy School of Government, report that investors disregard the costs of actively managed plans, focusing instead on annualized returns, which do not predict future performance.[17] The attention paid to past performance is a behavior that leads to misguided choices. The authors find no indication that nonportfolio services justify the higher fees their managers charge investors. Moreover, they find that investors with high financial literacy tend to pay low fees.

Familiarity Bias

People prefer to invest in what is familiar, favoring their own country, region, state, and company. Behavioral finance specialists characterize this preference as "familiarity bias." In "Familiarity Breeds Investment," Gur Huberman, a professor of behavioral finance at Columbia University's Graduate School of Business, finds that in 49 out of 50 states, investors are more likely to hold shares of their local Regional Bell Operating Company (RBOC) than of any other single RBOC.[18] The preference of investors for companies from their region is a narrow form of geographic bias; preference for domestic companies over international ones is a widely held preference known as "equity home bias." In "Understanding the Equity Home Bias: Evidence from Survey Data," Norman Strong, of the University of Manchester in the United Kingdom, and Xinzhong Xu, affiliated with Peking University, investigate the equity-home-bias puzzle—why do investors tend to favor their own country's equities, despite the advantages of international diversification?[19] However, Strong and Xu argue that, by itself, investors' relative optimism about the home market cannot explain equity home bias. In their view, fund sponsors who constrain fund managers or measure their performance against domestic benchmarks may influence fund managers to invest in domestic equities.

A widespread and particularly dangerous form of familiarity bias is employees' preference for investing in their employer's stock. Employees already have a stake in the performance of their companies without including company shares in their investment portfolios. Not only does concentration in one asset violate the principle of portfolio diversification, but, if employees devote a large portion of their portfolios to their own company's shares, they run the risk of compounding their suffering if the company does poorly: first, in loss of compensation and job security, and second, in loss of retirement savings. This is exactly what happened to employees at Enron and Fannie Mae, when Enron filed for bankruptcy in 2001 and when Fannie Mae was placed into government conservatorship in 2008. In "Are Empowerment and Education Enough? Underdiversification in 401(k) Plans," James J. Choi, David Laibson, and Brigitte C. Madrian, who at the time of publication were professors at Yale, Harvard, and the University of Pennsylvania, respectively, contend that employees invest in company stock for a variety of reasons, including familiarity bias, loyalty to their employers, naive-diversification strategies, and passivity.[20] Employers share some of the blame for these patterns, encouraging such behavior through employee stock-ownership plans

(ESOPs) and employers' matching contributions. The preference for glamour stocks (high-growth, well-known, trendy stocks), another form of familiarity bias, is discussed in the following section on growth investing.

Manias and Panics

Financial mania is the rapid rise in the price of an asset, reflecting a high degree of collective enthusiasm or exuberance regarding that asset's prospects. Because a bubble inflates rapidly and is not durable, it is a common metaphor for financial mania. When the bubble bursts, the price of the asset plunges, setting off a panic. In "Financial Manias and Panics: A Socioeconomic Perspective," York University economist Brenda Spotton Visano uses sociologists' theories to shed light on the phenomena of mania and panic.[21] Visano describes financial mania as the "gradual spreading of speculative euphoria—one that becomes increasingly intense."[22] She explains that mania occurs before, and panic occurs after, "the peak of the business cycle spawned by revolutionary innovation."[23] Referring to sociological theories, Visano traces the progression of financial speculation and innovation from "optimistic uncertainty" to a "swell of speculative excitement" to "apparent and estimable" innovation. Unfounded optimism can lead to eventual distress and possible panic. In the past 10 years, two instances of mania followed by panic have severely harmed investors: the bursting of the dotcom bubble in 2000 and the housing crisis, which became acute in 2008 and is continuing. A diversified portfolio, including fixed-income securities, would have mitigated the impact of these crises on investment portfolios.

Momentum Investing

Momentum investing is an investment strategy whereby the investor buys securities with high recent returns and sells those with low recent returns, in the expectation that past trends will continue. Mohacsy and Lefer equate momentum investing, which is a manifestation of magical thinking and herd behavior, with the Greater Fool Theory.[24] Momentum investing can give rise to speculative bubbles, such as the dot-com bubble of the second half of the 1990s. In the article, "A Unified Theory of Underreaction, Momentum Trading, and Overreaction in Asset Markets," Harrison Hong and Jeremy C. Stein, who were business school professors at Stanford and the Massachusetts

Institute of Technology, respectively, when they wrote this article, show that short-run momentum can lead to long-run reversals when stock prices overshoot their intrinsic value.[25] They distinguish between "newswatchers," who focus on privately observed information, and "momentum traders," who seek to take advantage of a price trend. Both are subject to bounded rationality,[26] not taking into account all publicly available information. Newswatchers focus on information that may spread slowly, giving momentum traders an opportunity to step in and to trigger an overreaction followed by a reversal. Slow information diffusion is characteristic of small-cap stocks with low analyst coverage.

Naive Diversification

In their study, "Naive Diversification Strategies in Defined Contribution Saving Plans," Benartzi and Thaler explore the tendency of investors in defined contribution retirement plans to take the "naive diversification" approach toward asset allocation.[27] In other words, if given *n* options, investors allocate their assets proportionally among them, so that each option receives *1/n* of the total. The authors maintain that, although naive diversification is not necessarily a bad approach for unsophisticated investors, this method may prove costly if the employer provides a poor selection of choices. The study implies that employers should design retirement plans carefully, to produce a scenario in which naive diversification becomes an effective strategy.

Noise Trading

As a technical term, "noise" refers to false signals and short-term volatility that obscure the overall trend. Therefore, "noise trading" describes the activities of "an investor who makes decisions regarding buy and sell trades without the use of fundamental data. These investors generally have poor timing, follow trends, and overreact to good and bad news."[28] In "All that Glitters: The Effect of Attention and News on the Buying Behavior of Individual and Institutional Investors," Brad M. Barber and Terrance Odean show that although individual investors are net buyers of attention-grabbing stocks—stocks that are in the news or that experience abnormal one-day returns or trading volumes—these stocks subsequently do not perform as well as the stocks that the same investors decided to sell.[29] This research suggests that day trading is not a worthwhile activity.

Underdiversification

Behavioral finance theorists do not have a monopoly on identifying investing mistakes. Inadequate portfolio diversification, for example, violates the principles of best practice set out in Modern Portfolio Theory, which Nobel Prize–winning economist Harry Markowitz developed in the 1950s. Meir Statman, a professor of finance at Santa Clara University, explored the lack of diversification in U.S. investors' equity portfolios. Although mean-variance portfolio theory recommends that portfolios hold at least 300 stocks, the average investor actually holds only three or four, representing an extremely underdiversified portfolio. The typical investor's concentration in employer, large-capitalization, and domestic stocks also works against the advantages of diversification.[30]

A contrarian view of portfolio diversification is found in "Portfolio Concentration and the Performance of Individual Investors," by finance professors Zoran Ivković, of Michigan State University, Clemens Sialm, of the University of Texas at Austin, and Scott Weisbenner, of the University of Illinois at Urbana-Champaign.[31] The authors determine that, contrary to conventional financial advice recommending investment in well-diversified portfolios, some individual investors (particularly those from households with large portfolios) achieve superior returns by concentrating their investments in a few stocks. Financial returns in excess of the norm correlate with local stocks, stocks not included in the S&P 500 index (small capitalization stocks), and stocks with less analyst coverage.

Other Behavioral Patterns

Behavioral finance specialists have also analyzed other investment patterns that are the frequent object of debate. Two of them are the appropriateness of annuity investing and the relative merit of the growth vs. value styles of investing.

Annuity Investing

To suggest that all annuities are poor investments is unjustified. However, according to the article, "Who Chooses Annuities? An Experimental Investigation of the Role of Gender, Framing and Defaults," by Julie R. Agnew, Lisa R. Anderson, and Lisa R. Szykman, of the College of William and Mary, and Jeffrey R. Gerlach of the Massachusetts Institute of Technology, annuities offer modest returns for a given level of risk. The authors note that annuities attract a middle-class, relatively well-educated, and predominantly female clientele, motivated by affective (emotional) factors, such as trust, familiarity, and loss aversion. Examining how women and men differ in their approach to the choice of whether to purchase an annuity or to invest on their own, and controlling for risk aversion and financial literacy, the authors find that women are more likely than men to purchase an annuity.[32] Although men tend to overconfidence in their investing prowess, perhaps this trait may have a benefit; instead, women settle for modest annuity-like returns.

Growth Investing

In the "value style" of investing, an investor buys out-of-favor stocks with low price-to-earnings and price-to-book value ratios, stocks that the investor believes are trading below their intrinsic value. "Growth style" describes an approach to investing that focuses on high-growth stocks, even if they have high price-to-earning ratios. To imply that growth investing is an investing mistake would be an overstatement. However, an investor's choice of growth- or value-investing styles may affect the outcome of his or her results. In their article, "Value and Growth Investing: Review and Update," Louis K. C. Chan and Josef Lakonishok, both finance professors at the University of Illinois at Urbana-Champaign, maintain that value investing generates superior returns to growth investing, particularly for small-capitalization stocks.[33] The authors' assertion carries a significant caveat: before 1990, value stocks had a superior performance, but their performance reversed during the 1990s. The authors attribute the reversal during that decade to investors' excessive enthusiasm for technology, media, and telecom stocks that defied economic logic.

The authors suggest that investors tend to underestimate the ability of value stocks to rebound and to overestimate the ability of glamour stocks to maintain above-average growth. Investors' overly optimistic tendency to project rapid growth rates into the future may have a cost, which is exacerbated by financial management agencies' practice of delegating investment decisions to professional money managers. Analysts, money managers, and pension plan executives often promote or invest in glamour stocks for a variety of inappropriate reasons that may betray the interests of their clients. Analysts may have conflicts of interests, relative to investment banking, leading them to recommend growth stocks; money managers may offer advice to investors that promote their own careers; and excitement over emerging technologies may lead advisers to select glamorous, but unwise, investments. Whether investor psychology or agency self-interest is the cause, excessive investment in these stocks may drive up the prices of growth stocks beyond their intrinsic value. This type of mispricing may persist for a long time but will not continue indefinitely; unappreciated value stocks eventually recover. Over time, growth stocks fail to meet optimistic expectations, while value stocks exceed pessimistic expectations.

CONCLUSION

By identifying and explaining patterns of poor investor decision making, behavioral finance theory has contributed to our understanding of investment behavior. In contrast to rational expectations theory, behavioral finance highlights the role of social, cognitive, and emotional factors in investing. Consequently, this field can help educate investors—an essential means of preventing investors from committing a predictable series of mistakes. In addition, the findings of behavioral scientists suggest that investors need streamlined, transparent investment disclosure, particularly in graphical format. Investment professionals should take into account the findings of behavioral finance when they advise clients and monitor their accounts. Finally, many scholars strongly advocate that employers improve their design of retirement plans to diversified, simple fund options and automatic enrollment provisions that require employees to opt out, in order to encourage participation.

BIBLIOGRAPHY

[1] Agnew, Julie R., Lisa R. Anderson, Jeffrey R. Gerlach & Lisa R. Szykman. (2008). "Who Chooses Annuities? An Experimental

Investigation of the Role of Gender, Framing and Defaults." *American Economic Review, 98*, no. 2 (May): 418–22. http://lrande.people.wm.edu/ http://lrande.people.wm.edu/links/AERP&P2008.pdf (accessed May 13, 2010).

[2] Barber, Brad M. & Terrance Odean. (2008). "All that Glitters: The Effect of Attention and News on the Buying Behavior of Individual and Institutional Investors." *Review of Financial Studies* 21, no. 2 (April): 785–818. Available by subscription: http://rfs. oxfordjournals.org/cgi/reprint/21/2/785 (January 5, 2010). Also available: http://faculty.haas.berkeley.edu/odean/papers/Attention/All%20that%20Glitters.pdf (accessed January 16, 2010).

[3] Barber, Brad M. & Terrance Odean. (2009). "Boys Will Be Boys: Gender, Overconfidence, and Common Stock Investment." *Quarterly Journal of Economics* 116, no. 1 (February 2001): 261–92. Available by subscription: http://www.jstor.org/stable/2696449 (accessed December 10). Also available: http://faculty.gsm.ucdavis.edu/~bmbarber/Paper%20Folder/QJE%20BoysWillBeBoys.pdf (accessed January 15, 2010).

[4] Barber, Brad M. & Terrance Odean. (1999). "The Courage of Misguided Convictions." *Financial Analysts Journal* 55, no. 6 (November–December): 41–55. Available by subscription: http://www.jstor.org/stable/4480208 (accessed December 10, 2009). Also available: http://faculty.haas.berkeley.edu/odean/Papers%20current%20versions/F*AJ%* 20NovDec99%20Barber%20and%20Odean.pdf (accessed January 15, 2010).

[5] Barber, Brad M. & Terrance Odean. (2002). "Online Investors: Do the Slow Die First?" Special issue, *Review of Financial Studies* 15, no. 2: 455–87. Available by subscription: http://www.jstor.org/stable/2696785 (accessed December 10, 2009). Also available: http://faculty.haas.berkeley.edu/odean/Papers%20current%20versions/Online%20RFS . pdf (accessed January 15, 2010).

[6] Barber, Brad M. & Terrance Odean. (2000). "Trading is Hazardous to Your Wealth: The Common Stock Investment Performance of Individual Investors." *Journal of Finance* 55, no. 2 (April): 773–806. Available by subscription: http://www.jstor.org/stable/222522 (December 10, 2009). Also available: http://faculty.haas.berkeley.edu/odean/Papers%20current%20versions/Individual _Investor _Performance _Final.pdf (accessed January 15, 2010).

[7] Benartzi, Shlomo & Richard H. Thaler. (1995). "Myopic Loss Aversion and the Equity Risk Premium." *Quarterly Journal of Economics* 110, no.

1 (February): 73–92. Available by subscription: http://www.jstor.org/stable/2118511 (accessed December 10, 2009).

[8] Benartzi, Shlomo & Richard H. Thaler. (2001). "Naive Diversification Strategies in Defined Contribution Saving Plans." *American Economic Review* 91, no. 1 (March): 79–98. Available by subscription: http://www.jstor.org/stable/2677899 (accessed December 10, 2009). Also available: http://faculty.chicagobooth.edu/richard.thaler/research/pdf/DiversificationStrategies.pdf (accessed January 15, 2010).

[9] Carhart, Mark M. (1997). "On Persistence in Mutual Fund Performance." *Journal of Finance* 52, no. 1 (March): 57–82. Available by subscription: http://www.jstor.org/stable/2329556 (accessed January 5, 2010).

[10] Chan, Louis K. C. & Josef Lakonishok. (2004). "Value and Growth Investing: Review and Update." *Financial Analysts Journal* 60, no. 1 (January–February): 7 1–86. Available by subscription: http://www.jstor.org/stable/4480542 (accessed January 12, 2010). Also available: http://www.lsvasset.com/pdf/Value-Review.pdf (accessed January 26, 2010).

[11] Choi, James J., David Laibson & Brigitte C. Madrian. (2005). "Are Empowerment and Education Enough? Underdiversification in 401(k) Plans." *Brookings Papers on Economic Activity*, no. *2, 15* 1–98. Available by subscription: http://www.jstor.org/stable/3805120 (accessed December 10, 2009) and https://muse.jhu.edu/journals/brookings_papers_ on_economic_activity/v2005/2005 .2choi.pdf (accessed January 15, 2010).

[12] Choi, James J., David Laibson & Brigitte C. Madrian. (2010). "Why Does the Law of One Price Fail? An Experiment on Index Mutual Funds." *Review of Financial Studies* 23, no. 4 (April). Available by subscription: http://www.nber.org/papers/w12261.pdf (accessed June 30, 2010). Also available: http://rfs.oxfordjournals.org/cgi/content/full/hhp097v1 (accessed January 25, 2010).

[13] Guiso, Luigi, Paola Sapienza & Luigi Zingales. (2008). "Trusting the Stock Market." *Journal of Finance* 63, no. 6 (December): 2557–2600. http://www.bus.wisc.edu/finance/Meyferth/Fedenia/Articles/Guiso%20Sapienza%20Zingales%202007.pdf (accessed May 19, 2010).

[14] Hong, Harrison & Jeremy C. Stein. (1999). "A Unified Theory of Underreaction, Momentum Trading, and Overreaction in Asset Markets." *Journal of Finance, 54*, no. 6 (December): 2143–84. http://www.economics harvard.edu/faculty/stein/files/UnifiedTheory.pdf

(accessed May 20, 2010).

[15] Huberman, Gur. (2001). "Familiarity Breeds Investment." *Review of Financial Studies* 14, no. 3 (Autumn): 659–80. Available by subscription: http://www.jstor.org/stable/2696769 (accessed December 10, 2009).

[16] Ivković, Zoran, Clemens Sialm & Scott Weisbenner. (2008). "Portfolio Concentration and the Performance of Individual Investors." *Journal of Financial and Quantitative Analysis, 43*, no. 3 (September): 613–56. Available by subscription: http://search.ebscohost.com/ (accessed January 5, 2010).

[17] Kahneman, Daniel & Mark W. Riepe. (1998). "Aspects of Investor Psychology." *Journal of Portfolio Management, 24*, no. 4 (Summer): 52. Available by subscription: http://find. galegroup.com/gtx/infomark. do?&contentSet=IAC-Documents&type=retrieve&tabID =T002&prodId=ITOF&docId=A21046822&source=gale&srcprod=ITO F&userGroup Name=loc_main&version=1 .0 (accessed June 29, 2010).

[18] Kahneman, Daniel & Amos Tversky. (1979). "Prospect Theory: An Analysis of Decision under Risk," *Econometrica*, 47, no. 2 (March): 279. Available by subscription: http://www.jstor. org/stable/1 914185 (accessed June 15, 2010).

[19] Mitchell, Olivia S. & Stephen P. Utkus. (2004). "Lessons from Behavioral Finance for Retirement Plan Design." In *Pension Design and Structure: New Lessons from Behavioral Finance*, edited by Olivia S. Mitchell and Stephen P. Utkus, 3–41. Oxford, UK: Oxford University Press. Version available at http://fic.wharton.upenn.edu/ fic/papers/03/03 34.pdf (accessed June 15, 2010).

[20] Mohacsy, Ildiko & Heidi Lefer. "Money and Sentiment: A Psychodynamic Approach to Behavioral Finance." *Journal of the American Academy of Psychoanalysis and Dynamic Psychiatry, 35*, no. 3 (Fall 2007): 455–75. Available by subscription from a number of vendors, including: http://proquest.umi.com/login (accessed January 13, 2010).

[21] Odean, Terrance. (1998). "Are Investors Reluctant to Realize Their Losses?" *Journal of Finance, 53*, no. 5 (October): 1775–98. Available by subscription: http://www.jstor.org/stable/ 117424 (accessed December 10, 2009). Also available: http://faculty.haas.berkeley.edu/ odean/Papers%20current%20versions/AreInvestorsReluctant.pdf (accessed January 15, 2010).

[22] Pressman, Steven. (1998). "On Financial Frauds and Their Causes:

Investor Overconfidence." *American Journal of Economics and Sociology, 57*, no. 4 (October): 405–21. Available by subscription: http://www.jstor.org/stable/3487115 (accessed December 10, 2009).

[23] Skinner, Jonathan. (2007). "Are You Sure You're Saving Enough for Retirement?" *Journal of Economic Perspectives, 21*, no. 3 (Summer): 59–80. Available by subscription: http://search. ebscohost.com/ (accessed January 5, 2010). Also available: http://www.dartmouth.edu/~ j skinner/documents/SkinnerAreyouSure.pdf (accessed January 15, 2010).

[24] Statman, Meir. (2004). "The Diversification Puzzle." *Financial Analysts Journal, 60*, no. 4 (July–August): 44–53. Available by subscription: http://www.jstor.org/stable/4480587 (accessed January 5, 2010).

[25] Strong, Norman & Xinzhong Xu. (2003). "Understanding the Equity Home Bias: Evidence from Survey Data." *Review of Economics and Statistics, 85*, no. 2 (May): 307–12. Available by subscription: http://www.jstor.org/stable/3211582 (accessed December 10, 2009).

[26] Van Rooij, Maarten, Annamaria Lusardi & Rob Alessie. (2007). "Financial Literacy and Stock Market Participation." National Bureau of Economic Research Working Paper 13565, October. http://www.nber. org/papers/w13565 (accessed May 21, 2010).

[27] Visano, Brenda Spotton. (2010). "Financial Manias and Panics: A Socioeconomic Perspective." *American Journal of Economics and Sociology, 61*, no. 4 (October 2002): 801–27. Available by subscription: http://www.jstor.org/stable/3487980 (accessed January 5).

End Notes

[1] Brad M. Barber and Terrance Odean, "The Courage of Misguided Convictions," *Financial Analysts Journal* 55, no. 6 (November–December 1999): 4 1–55. Available by subscription from JSTOR, *http://www.jstor.org/stable/* 4480208 (accessed December 10, 2009). Also available from http://faculty.haas.berkeley.edu/odean/Papers%20current%20versions/ FAJ%20NovDec99%20Barber%20and%20Odean.pdf (accessed January 15, 2010).

[2] Besides Barber and Odean, some of the major figures in the field of behavioral finance are Nicholas Barberis (Yale), Shlomo Benartzi (UCLA), David Hirshleifer (University of California at Irvine), Daniel Kahneman (Princeton), Andrei Shleifer (Harvard), Richard H. Thaler (University of Chicago), and Robert Vishny (University of Chicago).

[3] Daniel Kahneman and Mark W. Riepe, "Aspects of Investor Psychology," *Journal of Portfolio Management* 24, no. 4 (Summer 1998): 52. Available by subscription: http://find.galegroup. com/gtx/infomark.do?&contentSet=IAC-
Documents&type=retrieve&tabID=T002&prodId=ITOF&docId=A21
046822&source=gale&srcprod=ITOF& userGroupName=loc_main&version= 1.0 (accessed June 29, 2010).

[4] Steven Pressman, "On Financial Frauds and Their Causes: Investor Overconfidence," *American Journal of Economics and Sociology* 57, no. 4 (October 1998): 405–21. Available by subscription from JSTOR, http://www. jstor.org/stable/3487115 (accessed December 10, 2009).

[5] Ildiko Mohacsy and Heidi Lefer, "Money and Sentiment: A Psychodynamic Approach to Behavioral Finance," *Journal of the American Academy of Psychoanalysis and Dynamic Psychiatry* 35, no. 3 (Fall 2007): 455–75. Available by subscription from a number of vendors, including Proquest, *http://proquest.umi.com/login* (accessed January 13, 2010).

[6] Olivia S. Mitchell and Stephen P. Utkus, "Lessons from Behavioral Finance for Retirement Plan Design," in *Pension Design and Structure: New Lessons from Behavioral Finance*, ed. Mitchell and Utkus, 3–41 (Oxford, UK: Oxford University Press, 2004).

[7] Maarten Van Rooij, Annamaria Lusardi, and Rob Alessie, "Financial Literacy and Stock Market Participation" (National Bureau of Economic Research Working Paper 13565, October 2007), *http://www.nber.org/papers/w13565* (accessed May 21, 2010).

[8] Annamaria Lusardi and Olivia S. Mitchell, "Financial Literacy and Planning: Implications for Retirement Wellbeing" (Michigan Retirement Research Center Research Paper No. WP 2005-108, December 2005), 1–28, http://papers.ssrn.com/sol3/papers.cfm?abstract_id=881847 (accessed May 24, 2010).

[9] Luigi Guiso, Paola Sapienza, and Luigi Zingales, "Trusting the Stock Market," *Journal of Finance* 63, no. 6 (December 2008): 2557–2600, http://www.bus.wisc.edu/finance/ Meyferth/Fedenia/Articles/Guiso%20Sapienza% 20Zingales%202007.pdf (accessed May 19, 2010).

[10] Jonathan Skinner, "Are You Sure You're Saving Enough for Retirement?" *Journal of Economic Perspectives* 21, no. 3 (Summer 2007): 59–80. Available by subscription from EBSCO, http://search.ebscohost.com/ (accessed January 5, 2010). Also available from http://www.dartmouth.edu/~jskinner/documents/SkinnerAreyouSure.pdf (accessed January 15, 2010).

[11] Brad M. Barber and Terrance Odean, "Trading Is Hazardous to Your Wealth: The Common Stock Investment Performance of Individual Investors," *Journal of Finance* 55, no. 2 (April 2000): 773–806. Available by subscription from JSTOR, http://www.jstor.org/stable/2 22522 *(accessed December 10, 2009). Also available from* http://faculty. haas.berkeley.edu/odean/Papers%20current%20versions/Individual_Investor_Performance_ Final.pdf (accessed January 15, 2010).

[12] Brad M. Barber and Terrance Odean, "Boys Will Be Boys: Gender, Overconfidence, and Common Stock Investment," *Quarterly Journal of Economics* 116, no. 1 (February 2001): 261–92. Available by subscription from JSTOR, *http://www.jstor.org/stable/2696449* (accessed December 10, 2009). Also available from http://faculty.gsm. ucdavis.edu/~bmbarber/Paper%20Folder/QJE%20BoysWillBeBoys.pdf (accessed January 15, 2010).

[13] Brad M. Barber and Terrance Odean, "Online Investors: Do the Slow Die First?" Special issue, *Review of Financial Studies* 15, no. 2 (2002): 455–87. Available by subscription from JSTOR, http://www.jstor.org/stable/ 2696785 (accessed December 10, 2009). Also available from http://faculty.haas.berkeley.edu/odean/Papers% 20current%20versions/ Online%20RFS.pdf (accessed January 15, 2010).

[14] Terrance Odean, "Are Investors Reluctant To Realize Their Losses?" *Journal of Finance* 53, no. 5 (October 1998): 1775–98. Available by subscription from JSTOR, http://www.jstor.org/stable/117424 (accessed December 10, 2009). Also available from http://faculty.haas.berkeley.edu/odean/Papers%20current%20versions/ AreInvestorsReluctant.pdf (accessed January 15, 2010).

[15] Shlomo Benartzi and Richard H. Thaler, "Myopic Loss Aversion and the Equity Risk Premium," *Quarterly Journal of Economics* 110, no. 1 (February 1995): 73–92. Available by subscription from JSTOR, *http://www.jstor. org/stable/21* 18511 (accessed December 10, 2009); Shlomo Benartzi and Richard H. Thaler, "Risk Aversion or Myopia? Choices in

Repeated Gambles and Retirement Investments," *Management Science* 45, no. 3 (March 1999): 364–81. Available from several vendors by subscription, including JSTOR, http://www.jstor.org/stable/2634883 (accessed December 10, 2009).

[16] Mark M. Carhart, "On Persistence in Mutual Fund Performance," *Journal of Finance* 52, no. 1 (March 1997): 57– 82. Available by subscription from JSTOR, http://www.jstor.org/stable/2329556 (accessed January 5, 2010).

[17] James J. Choi, David Laibson, and Brigitte C. Madrian, "Why Does the Law of One Price Fail? An Experiment on Index Mutual Funds," *Review of Financial Studies* 23, no. 4 (April 2010): 1405. Available by subscription from National Bureau of Economic Research, http://www.nber.org/papers/w12261.pdf (accessed June 30, 2010). Also available from Oxford Journals, http://rfs.oxfordjournals.org/cgi/content/ full/hhp097v1 (accessed January 25, 2010).

[18] Gur Huberman, "Familiarity Breeds Investment," *Review of Financial Studies* 14, no. 3 (Autumn 2001): 659–80. Available by subscription from JSTOR, http://www.jstor.org/stable/2696769 (accessed December 10, 2009).

[19] Norman Strong and Xinzhong Xu, "Understanding the Equity Home Bias: Evidence from Survey Data," *Review of Economics and Statistics* 85, no. 2 (May 2003): 307–12. Available by subscription from JSTOR, http://www. jstor.org/stable/3211582 (accessed December 10, 2009).

[20] James J. Choi, David Laibson, and Brigitte C. Madrian, "Are Empowerment and Education Enough? Underdiversification in 401(k) Plans," *Brookings Papers on Economic Activity* 2 (2005): 151–98. Available by subscription from JSTOR, http://www.jstor.org/stable/ 3805120 (accessed December 10, 2009) and Muse, https://muse.jhu.edu/journals/ brookings_papers_on_economic_activity/v2005/2005.2choi.pdf (accessed January 15, 2010).

[21] Brenda Spotton Visano, "Financial Manias and Panics: A Socioeconomic Perspective," *American Journal of Economics and Sociology* 61, no. 4 (October 2002): 801–27. Available by subscription from JSTOR, http://www. jstor.org/stable/3487980 (accessed January 5, 2010).

[22] Visano, "Financial Manias and Panics," 816.

[23] Visano, "Financial Manias and Panics," 809.

[24] Mohacsy and Lefer, "Money and Sentiment: A Psychodynamic Approach to Behavioral Finance."

[25] Harrison Hong and Jeremy C. Stein, "A Unified Theory of Underreaction, Momentum Trading, and Overreaction in Asset Markets," *Journal of Finance* 54, no. 6 (December 1999): 2143–84, http://www.economics.harvard.edu/ faculty/stein/files/UnifiedTheory.pdf (accessed May 20, 2010).

[26] According to BusinessDictionary. com, "bounded rationality" is the "concept that decision makers (irrespective of their level of intelligence) have to work under three unavoidable constraints: (1) only limited, often unreliable, information is available regarding possible alternatives and their consequences, (2) [the] human mind has only limited capacity to evaluate and process the information that is available, and (3) only a limited amount of time is available to make a decision. Therefore, even individuals who intend to make rational choices are bound to make satisficing (rather than maximizing or optimizing) choices in complex situations." "Bounded Rationality," BusinessDictionary. com, http://www.businessdictionary.com/definition/bounded-rationality.html (accessed June 18, 2010).

[27] Shlomo Benartzi and Richard H. Thaler, "Naive Diversification Strategies in Defined Contribution Saving Plans," *American Economic Review* 91, no. 1 (March 2001): 79–98. Available by subscription from JSTOR, http://www. jstor.org/stable/2677899 (accessed December 10, 2009). Also available from http://faculty.chicagobooth.edu/ richard.thaler/ research/pdf/ (accessed January 15, 2010).

[28] "Noise Trader," *Investopedia*, http://www.investopedia.com/terms/n/noisetrader.asp (accessed June 18, 2010).

[29] Brad M. Barber and Terrance Odean, "All that Glitters: The Effect of Attention and News on the Buying Behavior of Individual and Institutional Investors," *Review of Financial Studies* 21, no. 2 (April 2008): 785–818. Available by subscription from Oxford Journals, http://rfs.oxfordjournals.org/cgi/reprint/21/2/785 (accessed January 5, 2010). Also available from http://faculty.haas.berkeley.edu/odean/papers/Attention/All%20that%20Glitters.pdf (accessed January 16, 2010).

[30] Meir Statman, "The Diversification Puzzle," *Financial Analysts Journal* 60, no. 4 (July–August 2004): 44–53. Available by subscription from JSTOR, http://www.jstor.org/stable/4480587 (accessed January 5, 2010).

[31] Zoran Ivković, Clemens Sialm, and Scott Weisbenner, "Portfolio Concentration and the Performance of Individual Investors," *Journal of Financial and Quantitative Analysis* 43, no. 3 (September 2008): 613–56. Available by subscription from EBSCO, http://search.ebscohost.com/ (accessed January 5, 2010).

[32] Julie R. Agnew, Lisa R. Anderson, Jeffrey R. Gerlach, and Lisa R. Szykman, "Who Chooses Annuities? An Experimental Investigation of the Role of Gender, Framing and Defaults," *American Economic Review* 98, no. 2 (May 2008): 418–22, http://lrande.people.wm.edu/links/AERP&P2008.pdf (accessed May 13, 2010).

[33] Louis K. C. Chan and Josef Lakonishok, "Value and Growth Investing: Review and Update," *Financial Analysts Journal* 60, no. 1 (January–February 2004): 71–86. Available by subscription: http://www.jstor.org/stable/4480542_(accessed January 12, 2010). Also available: http://www.lsvasset.com/pdf/Value-Review.pdf (accessed January 26, 2010).

In: Investor Behavior: Patterns and Pitfalls
Editors: Andre Moliére
ISBN: 978-1-61470-205-4

Chapter 2

Annotated Bibliography on the Behavioral Characteristics of U.S. Investors

Federal Research Division and Library of Congress

Summary

Investor behavior is a hotly debated topic within the academic community. One relatively new area of study is the field of behavioral finance, which highlights departures from rational behavior in investing. Behavioral finance theory poses a challenge to many of the long- established assumptions of the rational expectations school of thought, which posits that people (investors) maximize utility (returns), acting rationally and in their self-interest. By focusing on the psychological and behavioral elements in the determination of stock prices, behavioral finance also challenges the efficient market hypothesis (EMH), which holds that market prices reflect all known information. EMH, developed by University of Chicago economist and Nobel Laureate Eugene Fama, implies that beating the market by identifying undervalued securities is impossible. Whether EMH remains valid is beyond the scope of this annotated bibliography, which is more concerned with investor behavior than with market efficiency. In other words, how the market behaves is not relevant here. Instead, the focus of this bibliography is on how investors behave and on how investor education may help them avoid common mistakes. This bibliography covers the last 15 years.

This annotated bibliography draws primarily on the work of economists and finance professors, who support their conclusions with extensive statistical models based on actual investor activity. However, the bibliography also provides references from the social sciences, such as psychology and sociology, because behavioral finance is a multidisciplinary field, spanning a wide range of socioeconomic analyses. For example, risk aversion is related to the psychological concept of prospect theory. Princeton psychologist and Nobel Laureate Daniel Kahneman and the late psychologist Amos Tversky, who was last affiliated with Stanford University, developed prospect theory to explain how people maximize value or utility in choosing between alternatives that involve risk. Kahneman's article, "Aspects of Investor Psychology," co-authored with Charles Schwab executive Mark W. Riepe, is included in this bibliography.

The perspective of sociology is represented in the article, "Financial Manias and Panics: A Socioeconomic Perspective," by York University economist Brenda Spotton Visano, who shows how sociologists' theories shed light on the phenomena of manias and panics. Similarly, in the article, "On Financial Frauds and Their Causes: Investor Overconfidence," Steven Pressman, an economist at Monmouth University, maintains that empirical psychology, which analyzes how people make choices when confronted with uncertainty, offers a better explanation of how Ponzi schemes thrive than neoclassical economics, which emphasizes the role of asymmetric information in risky situations. Even neuroscience can illuminate investor behavior: in "Affect and Financial Decision-Making: How Neuroscience Can Inform Market Participants," a physician, Dr. Richard L. Peterson links risk avoidance and risk taking to separate brain systems.

The 52 abstracts in the bibliography are arranged according to the following categories, with the number of abstracted articles in each category provided in parentheses:

- 401(k) investing (9)
- Actively managed vs. indexed funds (3)
- Behavioral finance (16)
- Efficient market hypothesis (1)
- Institutional investing (3)
- Investing styles (2)
- Investment clienteles (2)
- Limited stock-market participation (2)
- Manias and panics (1)

- Mutual fund disclosure (3)
- Neuroscience and investing (1)
- Ponzi schemes (2)
- Portfolio diversification (2)
- Psychology and investing (2)
- Retirement saving adequacy (3)

Except for the three items on institutional investing, the articles focus on the behavior of individual retail investors, who could benefit from investor education.

Specialists in behavioral finance assert that many investors fall into predictable patterns of destructive behavior. Specifically, many investors damage their portfolios by underdiversifying; trading frequently; following the herd; favoring the familiar (domestic stocks, company stock, and glamour stocks); selling winning positions and holding onto losing positions (disposition effect); and succumbing to optimism, short-term thinking, and overconfidence (self-attribution bias). Scholars generally recommend investor education, although some doubt that it is effective. They propose careful design of defined-contribution retirement plans that encourage investors to make advantageous decisions and such related measures as opt-out participation, balanced investment options, and default asset allocations. They also recommend better mutual fund and 401(k) plan disclosure, particularly in graphical format, to combat the tendency of investors to place too much emphasis on prior fund performance and to overlook the long-term impact of fees.

The bibliography addresses a variety of other themes, such as the relative merit of actively managed funds and index funds; why many investors hold just a few stocks in an equity portfolio, instead of the roughly 300 required for diversification (investors are not always averse to risk, and some investments are regarded as lottery tickets); and how much money one should save for retirement, according to the life-cycle model of investing. The abstracted articles also profile investor clienteles for annuities and for stocks that yield high dividends. Although annuities offer modest returns on a risk-adjusted basis, they attract a middle-class, relatively well-educated, and predominantly female clientele, motivated by affective (emotional) factors, such as trust, familiarity, and loss aversion. Meanwhile, older and lower-income investors favor stocks with high-dividend yields and go so far as to time their investments to take into account dividend announcements and ex-dividend dates. Two abstracts discuss the impact of widespread financial illiteracy among the general public on retirement planning and stock-market participation. Lack of trust is identified as another factor discouraging stock-market participation.

Two abstracts deal with Ponzi schemes: Steven Pressman's article about financial frauds and a noteworthy article in the *CPA Journal*, "Recognizing the Red Flags of a Ponzi Scheme," by Sandra Benson, an attorney and a professor of business law at Middle Tennessee State University. In general, however, scholarly analyses of Ponzi schemes and affinity fraud appear to represent a gap in the academic literature.

ANNOTATED BIBLIOGRAPHY

401(k) Investing

Agnew, Julie, Pierluigi Balduzzi, and Annika Sundén. "Portfolio Choice and Trading in a Large 401(k) Plan." *American Economic Review* 93, no. 1 (March 2003): 193–215. Available by subscription: http://www.jstor.org/stable/3132168 *(accessed December 10, 2009). Also available:* http://www2.bc.edu/~balduzzp/article16.pdf (accessed January 15, 2010).

Abstract: Professors Julie Agnew, of the College of William and Mary, and Pierluigi Balduzzi, of Boston College, and Annika Sundén, a research associate at the Center for Retirement Research at Boston College examine the behavior of those who invest in retirement accounts, rather than that of those who invest in discount brokerage accounts. Specifically, the authors analyze "nearly 7,000 401(k) accounts from a single plan for a period of more than four years, from April 1994 through August 1998," finding asset allocations that are "extreme" or "strongly bimodal" (with either 100 percent or 0 percent invested in equities). These allocations tend to be static. In addition, "equity allocations are higher for males, married investors, and for investors with higher earnings and more seniority on the job; equity allocations are lower for older investors." This research builds upon that of Brad M. Barber and Terrance Odean (for several articles describing Barber's and Odean's research, see the section, "Behavioral Finance"). However, in contrast to Barber's and Odean's discount brokerage sample, the investors in retirement accounts engage in very little trading activity or "portfolio reshuffling." Furthermore, the investors in retirement accounts do not exhibit the ability to time the market and do not react to market developments on the same day. Specifically, they do not take advantage of the "wildcard option" in equity mutual funds—an option to trade shares at stale prices that becomes available to investors because some stocks included in a mutual-fund portfolio do not trade in the last two hours of each day. The paper has five sections: (1) "Data," (2) "Allocations and Trading: Summary Statistics," (3) "Regression Analysis," (4) "The Timing and Changes in Equity Allocation," and (5) "Conclusion."

Benartzi, Shlomo. "Excessive Extrapolation and the Allocation of 401(k) Accounts to Company Stock." *Journal of Finance* 56, no. 5 (October 2001): 1747–64. Available by subscription: http://www.jstor.org/stable/2697737 (accessed January 5, 2010).

Abstract: Shlomo Benartzi, a business professor at the University of California at Los Angeles (UCLA), finds that participants in large retirement savings plans, including 401(k) plans, tend to invest a disproportionate percentage of their discretionary funds in company stock. In fact, at a Fortune 500 company, the employees' allocation to company stock reached 90 percent at the time this article was written. This finding contradicts the predictions of Harry Markowitz, who developed modern portfolio theory (MPT), and of William Sharpe, who developed the capital asset pricing model (CAPM), that people tend to hold diversified portfolios. Benartzi explores, as a potential explanation for investors' preference for company stock, the possibility that employees may excessively extrapolate past performance. Although the study confirms this behavior, Benartzi also concludes that allocations do not correlate to future returns. Thus, he rules out an information-based explanation. Benartzi also explores other behavioral explanations, namely investor optimism, overconfidence, and familiarity. Finally, the author finds that employees with lower levels of education tend not to understand the risk associated with investing in company stock. Benartzi relies on the data provided in the 1993 annual reports to the SEC of employee stock purchases (11-k filings), as well as on surveys of subscribers to the market information service *Morningstar.com* and on surveys of UCLA employees. The paper has three sections: (1) "Data," (2) "Excessive Extrapolation and Company Stock," and (3) "Summary and Conclusions."

Benartzi, Shlomo, and Richard H. Thaler. "Heuristics and Biases in Retirement Savings Behavior." *Journal of Economic Perspectives* 21, no. 3 (Summer 2007): 81–104. Available by subscription: http://search.ebscohost.com/ (accessed January 5, 2010).

Abstract: In this article, pioneering academics in the field of behavioral finance, Shlomo Benartzi of UCLA and Richard Thaler of the University of Chicago, systematically examine the decision- making process of employees investing in retirement plans. Rejecting the assumptions of standard economic theories of saving, which posit investor rationality, the authors identify heuristics (rules of thumb) and biases that shape investor choices. For example, according to the mental accounting heuristic, investors distinguish between "old money" and "new money," investing these types of funds differently. The authors approach the topic systematically, examining a series of discrete decisions that investors make: whether or not to enroll in retirement plans, how much to contribute, how to allocate assets, and how to choose between defined benefit and defined contribution plans. Previous research demonstrates that employees are ill prepared to make any of these decisions, often responding passively, by not participating or by accepting default options. Therefore, the authors highlight several employer interventions that could help improve outcomes. They conclude that, both for sophisticated and for less sophisticated investors, the best interventions are the least expensive: "small changes in plan design, sensible default options, and opportunities to increase savings rates and rebalance portfolios automatically." The article is mostly descriptive and does not involve an original statistical study. The paper has six sections: (1) "Enrollment Decisions: To Join or Not to Join," (2) "Contribution Rates," (3) "Asset Allocation," (4) "Choosing between Defined Benefit and Defined Contribution Plans," (5) "Interventions by Plan Sponsors," and (6) "Conclusion."

Benartzi, Shlomo, and Richard H. Thaler. "Naïve Diversification Strategies in Defined Contribution Saving Plans." *American Economic Review* 91, no. 1 (March 2001): 79–98. Available by subscription: http://www.jstor.org/stable/2677899 (accessed December 10, 2009). Also available: http://faculty.chicagobooth.edu/richard.thaler/research/91010079.pdf (accessed January 15, 2010).

Abstract: UCLA finance professor Shlomo Benartzi and Richard H. Thaler, a finance professor at the University of Chicago, explore the tendency of many investors in defined contribution retirement plans to take the "naïve diversification" approach toward asset allocation. In other words, if given *n* options, investors allocate their assets proportionally among them, so that each option receives *1/n* of the total. Consistent with this approach, "the proportion invested in stocks depends strongly on the proportion of stock funds in the plan." A comparison of the asset allocation decisions made by two groups with different retirement plans—pilots at TWA and employees of the University of California—demonstrates the impact on overall asset allocation patterns when many participants behave in this way. The authors survey employees of the University of California, using hypothetical questionnaires and examining cross-sectional data on retirement savings plans (derived from a database covering 170 mostly corporate retirement plans). Confirming the initial finding, the authors maintain that, although naïve diversification is not necessarily a bad approach for unsophisticated investors, this method may prove costly if the employer provides a poor selection of choices or does not anticipate participants choosing this way. In addition, "results suggest that the increase in retirement funds invested in equities over the past decade may be partly explained by the abundance of new equity funds that have been added to these plans (though the booming stock market in the 1 990s has also been an important factor)." The paper has three sections: (1) "Experimental Evidence on the Diversification Heuristic," (2) "Does the Array of Funds Offered Affect Participants' Choices?" and (3) "Summary and Discussion."

Choi, James J., David Laibson, and Brigitte C. Madrian. "Are Empowerment and Education Enough? Underdiversification in 401(k) Plans." *Brookings Papers on Economic Activity* 2 (2005): 15 1–98. Available by subscription: http://www.jstor.org/stable/3805120 (accessed December 10, 2009) and https://muse.jhu.edu/journals/brookings_papers_ on_economic_ activity/v2005/2005 .2choi.pdf (accessed January 15, 2010).

Abstract: At the time of the article's publication, James J. Choi, David Laibson, and Brigitte C. Madrian were professors at Yale, Harvard, and the University of Pennsylvania, respectively. The authors explore the tendency of employees to invest in company stock in their 401(k) plans, despite the risks associated with the resulting underdiversification. Employees invest in company stock for a variety of reasons, including familiarity bias, loyalty to their employers, naïve diversification strategies, and passivity. Employers share some of the blame for these patterns, encouraging such behavior through employee stock ownership plans (ESOP) and employer matching contributions. Regulation of this type of investment is also lax. Specifically, the Employee Retirement Income Security Act of 1974 (ERISA) does not restrict investments in company stock in defined contribution plans to the same extent that it does for defined benefit plans. In fact, "current 401(k) regulations allow companies to severely restrict their employees' diversification out of employer stock." The authors find that even when holding requirements were relaxed at five companies, "it was typical for over 90 percent of employer match balances to remain in employer stock." Similarly, investor education and news stories about the financial calamities experienced by employees at such companies as Enron, WorldCom, and Global Crossing have had a minimal impact on investor behavior. These findings demonstrate that a combination of "empowerment and education" does not substantially help. The authors recommend that "default asset allocation for employer matching contributions [be] changed to provide greater diversification" by requiring them "to meet the same fiduciary standards that apply to defined-benefit plans." The paper has five sections: (1) "Regulation of Employer Stockholding in 401(k) Plans," (2) "Previous Research on Employer Stock in 401(k) Plans," (3) "Employee-Level Data on 401(k) Participation," (4) "Empowerment: The Effect of Relaxing Diversification Restrictions," and (5) "Education: The Effect of Enron, WorldCom, and Global Crossing."

Choi, James J., David Laibson, Brigitte C. Madrian, and Andrew Metrick. "Defined Contribution Pensions: Plan Rules, Participant Choices, and the Path of Least Resistance." *Tax Policy and the Economy* 16 (2002): 67–113. Available by subscription: http://www.jstor.org/stable/20140495 (accessed December 10, 2009) and http://www.nber.org/papers/ w8655 .pdf (accessed January 15, 2010).

Abstract: At the time of this article's publication, authors Choi and Laibson were professors at Harvard, Madrian was a professor at the University of Chicago, and Andrew Metrick was a professor at University of Pennsylvania. The authors examine the behavior of employees toward 401(k) plans, including savings rates and asset allocation. After examining the anonymous administrative records of several large firms that collectively employ almost 200,000 individuals, they find a tendency toward passive decision making and the "path of least resistance." For example, "automatic enrollment results in many participants remaining at the employer-specified default for both the contribution rate and asset allocation." In addition, there is a "disturbing" tendency to hold large balances in employer stock. Therefore, the authors conclude that employers bear a serious responsibility to design 401(k) plans in such a way that they optimize outcomes for participants. They review in detail seven features of 401(k) plans, which affect savings rates: eligibility, matching, automatic enrollment, choices of asset allocation, financial education in the workplace, automatic increases in the contribution rate, and automatic cash distributions for terminated employees with low account balances. The authors find that financial education has a positive, but limited impact on the quality of investment choices. The paper has six sections: (1) "Executive Summary," (2) "Introduction," (3) "Savings Adequacy," (4) "Seven Institutional Features of 401(k) Plans," (5) "Conclusions," and (6) appendices ("Appendix A: Data" and "Appendix B: 401(K)-Plan Participant Satisfaction Survey Questions").

Madrian, Brigitte C., and Dennis F. Shea. "The Power of Suggestion: Inertia in 401(k) Participation and Savings Behavior." *Quarterly Journal of Economics* 116, no. 4 (November 2001): 1149–87. Available by subscription: *http://www.jstor.org/stable/* 2696456 (accessed January 5, 2010). Also available: http://www.retirementmadesimpler. org/Library/The%20Power% 20of%20Suggestion-%20Inertia% 20in%2040 1 (k).pdf (accessed January 15, 2010).

Abstract: At the time she co-authored this article, Brigitte C. Madrian was an economics professor at the University of Chicago. Currently, she is a professor of public policy and corporate management at Harvard. Dennis F. Shea is the head of executive compensation strategy and client services at Aetna. Analyzing "the impact of automatic enrollment on 401(k) savings behavior," based on an examination of the behavior of participants in the 401(k) plan at a large U.S. corporation that adopted an automatic enrollment policy, the authors arrive at two conclusions. They find that automatic enrollment leads to significantly higher participation, but automatic enrollment causes many participants to "retain both the default contribution rate and fund allocation." The authors attribute these tendencies to inertia, to "the power of suggestion," and to the employees' perception that the default contribution rates and allocations represent investment advice. They point out that such behavior has implications for the design of 401(k) and other retirement savings plans, as well as indicating how economic and noneconomic factors influence individual savings choices. The authors recommend making investment choices less complicated and providing investor education, to combat the inclination of potential investors to procrastinate about saving. Investor education could also encourage employees to opt for higher contribution rates and more aggressive investment strategies. The paper has seven sections: (1) "Introduction," (2) "Features of the 401(k) Savings Plan at a Large U.S. Corporation," (3) "The Data," (4) "The Effect of Automatic Enrollment on

401(k) Participation, Contribution Rates, and Fund Allocations," (5) "The 'Default' Effect of Automatic Enrollment," (6) "Explaining the Effect of Automatic Enrollment on 401(k) Savings Behavior," and (7) "Conclusions."

Mitchell, Olivia S., and Stephen P. Utkus. "Lessons from Behavioral Finance for Retirement Plan Design." In *Pension Design and Structure—New Lessons from Behavioral Finance*. Oxford, UK: Oxford University Press, 2004, 3–41.

Abstract: Olivia Mitchell of the University of Pennsylvania and Stephen Utkus of the Vanguard Group summarize the key findings of research conducted from the perspective of behavioral finance by the Pension Research Council at the University of Pennsylvania on pension design and structure. The article begins by examining the fundamental issue of how people make the economic decision to save for retirement in the first place. Moving beyond conventional wisdom on the rational allocation of resources over a lifetime, they highlight miscalculations made by savers as a result of bounded rationality and self-control. They label those who are prone to defer consumption as "exponential discounters" and those who save little or nothing as "hyperbolic discounters," reflecting different subjective discount rates applied to the time value of money. Individuals also depart from conventional economic theory by being heavily influenced by the framing of retirement saving decisions. It is particularly noteworthy that automatic enrollment leads to much higher participation rates, as individuals tend to acquiesce by participating and accepting whatever default options the plan provides. By the same token, when required to opt into a retirement plan, many individuals tend to procrastinate or do nothing (inertia). The authors challenge the assumption that actual investor practice conforms to Modern Portfolio Theory (MPT), which posits that investors are sophisticated enough to weigh risk-reward trade-offs carefully when designing a portfolio. The preference for employee stock is an example of suboptimal diversification. Other pitfalls are overreliance on past performance as a predictor of future performance, overconfidence, and loss aversion. The authors believe that prospect theory, which emphasizes the role of incremental gains and losses rather than wealth maximization, offers a better explanation than does MPT for how investors measure utility under conditions of uncertainty. The authors also examine the decumulation phase, when retirees tap into their savings. In conclusion, the authors recommend that companies take the lessons of behavioral finance into account when designing retirement plans. The chapter has four sections: 1)

"The Decision to Save," 2) "The Investment Decision," 3) "The Decumulation Decision," and 4) "Policy and Plan Design Alternatives."

Morrin, Maureen, Susan Broniarczyk, J. Jeffrey Inman, and John Broussard. "Saving for Retirement: The Effects of Fund Assortment Size and Investor Knowledge on Asset Allocation Strategies." *Journal of Consumer Affairs* 42, no. 2 (Summer 2008): 206–22. Available by subscription from a number of vendors including: http://proquest.umi.com/ login (accessed January 5, 2010).

Abstract: Rutgers University professors Maureen Morrin and John Broussard teach marketing and finance, respectively. Susan Broniarczyk of the University of Texas and J. Jeffrey Inman of the University of Pittsburgh are both marketing professors. The authors explore the choices that 401(k) investors make when allocating assets among the three categories of mutual funds—equity, bond, and money market—given variations in the assortment of available funds. They conduct a decision-simulation study among 211 adults asked to make 401(k) investments, in cases in which the number of funds varies from three to 21. Controlling for the proportion of funds offered within each asset class, the authors find that less knowledgeable investors, faced with more choices of funds, demonstrate a statistically significant shift in assets from bond funds to stock funds. The authors' explanation for this phenomenon is that less knowledgeable investors apparently have difficulty distinguishing among bond funds and perceive that equity funds offer more variety. By contrast, since knowledgeable investors understand the benefits of diversification, they tend to adhere to asset-allocation goals. As a solution, the authors advocate that 401(k) plans provide automatic enrollment, unless an employee decides to opt out, along with balanced default options for asset allocation. The opt-out provision would correct the tendency of some less knowledgeable investors not to participate for various reasons, such as a lack of confidence or confusion caused by too many options. The paper has five sections: 1) "Assortment," (2) "Knowledge," (3) "Method," (4) "Results," and (5) "Discussion."

Actively Managed vs. Indexed Funds

Baks, Klaas P., Andrew Metrick, and Jessica Wachter. "Should Investors Avoid All Actively Managed Mutual Funds? A Study in Bayesian

Performance Evaluation." *Journal of Finance* 56, no. 1 (February 2001): 45–85. Available by subscription: http://www.jstor. org/stable/222463 (accessed December 10, 2009). Also available: http://finance.wharton. upenn.edu/ ~rlwctr/papers/9918.pdf (accessed January 15, 2010).

Abstract: Klaas P. Baks and Andrew Metrick are finance professors at the University of Pennsylvania; Jessica Wachter is a finance professor at New York University. The authors explore whether investing in actively managed funds is ever in investors' interest, or whether investors should avoid them altogether. Actively managed funds carry higher fees and transaction costs than index funds. A related issue is whether actively managed funds outperform the benchmarks that index funds track. In statistical terms, this means that some managers may have a record of producing a positive alpha (beating the benchmark). The authors specifically study the "portfolio-choice problem for the mean-variance investor choosing among a risk-free asset, index funds, and actively managed mutual funds." They use Bayesian statistics to examine investors' prior beliefs about managerial skill, applying this methodology to a sample of 1,437 mutual funds. The authors conclude that the "case against investing in actively managed mutual funds cannot rest solely on the available statistical evidence." The paper has five sections: (1) "The Investor's Problem and Prior Beliefs," (2) "Bayesian Performance Evaluation and Portfolio Choice," (3) "Empirical Results," (4) "Conclusion," and (5) appendices ("Appendix A. Posterior Distribution and Expectation of *a*," "Appendix B. Predictive Return and Factor Distribution," and "Appendix C. The Portfolio-Choice Problem and the Positive-Investment Condition").

Carhart, Mark M. "On Persistence in Mutual Fund Performance." *Journal of Finance* 52, no. 1 (March 1997): 57–82. Available by subscription: http://www.jstor.org/stable/2329556 (accessed January 5, 2010).

Abstract: Mark M. Carhart wrote this article when he was a professor of finance at the University of Southern California; he later worked at Goldman Sachs and Global Alpha, managing hedge funds. Carhart examines persistence (relative strength) in mutual-fund performance, in terms of mean and risk-adjusted returns. He analyzes a database of diversified equity mutual funds for the period from January 1962 to December 1993, taking care to eliminate survivorship bias (the disappearance of unsuccessful funds from a performance index). Using the capital asset pricing model (CAPM) and four-factor regression to isolate the causes of performance, he finds that following a momentum strategy (buying securities with high recent returns and selling those with low recent returns, in the expectation that past trends will continue) does not lead to higher returns. However, significant persistence is "concentrated in strong underperformance by the worst-return mutual funds." In general, evidence does not support the "existence of skilled or informed portfolio managers." The author concludes with practical advice for mutual fund investors: "(1) Avoid funds with persistently poor performance; (2) funds with high returns last year have higher-than-average expected returns next year, but not in years thereafter; and (3), the investment costs of expense ratios, transaction costs, and load fees all have a direct negative impact on performance." The paper has six sections: (1) "Data," (2) "Models of Performance Measurement," (3) "Persistence in One-Year Return-Sorted Mutual Fund Portfolios," (4) "Interpreting the Performance on Past-Winner Mutual Funds," (5) "Longer-Term Persistence in Mutual Fund Portfolios," and (6) "Conclusion."

Choi, James J., David Laibson, and Brigitte C. Madrian. "Why Does the Law of One Price Fail? An Experiment on Index Mutual Funds." *Review of Financial Studies* (November 14, 2009). Available by subscription: http://www.nber.org/ /papers/w1 2261 .pdf (accessed January 16, 2010). Also available: http://rfs.oxfordjournals.org/cgi/content/full/hhp097v1 (accessed January 25, 2010).

Abstract: At the time of this article's publication, Choi, Laibson, and Madrian were professors at the Yale School of Management, Harvard's Department of Economics, and Harvard's Kennedy School of Government, respectively. Investigating why individuals invest in high-fee index funds, the authors find that these investors base their decisions on annualized returns since inception, even though these returns do not predict future returns. The authors find no indication that nonportfolio services justify the higher fees they charge investors. Moreover, they find that higher financial literacy correlates with lower fees paid. Investors who lack financial knowledge often sense they are making a mistake. The results of this study indicate the need for investor education regarding fees paid for mutual fund investments. The researchers asked "730 experimental subjects to each allocate a hypothetical $10,000 among four real [Standard & Poor (S&P)] 500 index funds." The subject pool comprised Harvard staff members, MBA students at the Wharton School of Business, and college students recruited on the Harvard campus. In making their allocations, the subjects of the study relied on the funds' prospectuses and took into account expected payments linked to performance incentives. Appendices provide the material distributed to subjects. The paper has seven sections: (1) "S&P 500 Index Fund Experiment Design," (2) "Subject Characteristics," (3) "Main Experimental Results," (4) "Interpretation," (5) "Relationship between Portfolio Choices and Subject Characteristics," (6) "Conclusion," and (7) appendices.

Behavioral Finance

Baker, Malcolm, and Jeffrey Wurgler. "Investor Sentiment in the Stock Market." *The Journal of Economic Perspectives* 21, no. 2 (spring 2007): 129–51. http://www.people.hbs.edu/ mbaker/cv/papers/InvestorSentiment.pdf (accessed January 12, 2010).

Abstract: Malcolm Baker is a finance professor at Harvard Business School, and Jeffrey Wurgler is a finance professor at New York University's Stern School of Business. The authors maintain that stock market bubbles and crashes appear to confirm two assumptions of behavioral finance:

- Investors are subject to sentiment, or beliefs about cash flows and investment risks that are unjustified and contrary to the facts; and
- It is costly and risky to bet against sentimental investors.

Having accepted these two assumptions, the authors turn to two alternative models for measuring investor sentiment and its effects:

- "Bottom up," which focuses on such individual investor biases as overconfidence, representativeness (a behavioral shortcut that focuses excessively on recent events and returns), and conservatism; and
- "Top down," which focuses on aggregate or market-wide differences of opinion, sometimes in combination with restrictions on short sales.

The authors favor the top-down approach, although they believe that both deserve continued attention. They also believe that low-capitalization, non-dividend paying, unprofitable, distressed or potentially high-growth companies are more prone to investor sentiment than more established and reliably dividend-paying ("bond-like") companies because valuing the former is difficult and subjective. Such speculative securities are also more difficult to arbitrage, meaning to exploit and correct their mispricing, particularly given short-sale restraints on arbitrageurs. The authors demonstrate statistically that contrary to traditional financial theory, high beta stocks have lower rather than higher future average returns than bond-like stocks. The paper has six sections: (1) "Introduction," (2) "Theoretical effects of investor sentiment on stocks," (3) "Measuring investor sentiment," (4) "Using sentiment to explain current returns," (5) "Using sentiment to predict stock returns," and (6) "Conclusion."

Barber, Brad M., and Terrance Odean. "All that Glitters: The Effect of Attention and News on the Buying Behavior of Individual and Institutional Investors." *Review of Financial Studies* 21, no. 2 (April 2008): 785–818. Available by subscription: http://rfs. oxfordjournals.org/cgi/reprint/21/2/785 (January 5, 2010). Also available: http://faculty.haas.berkeley.edu/odean/papers/Attention/All%20that%20Glitters.pdf (accessed January 16, 2010).

Abstract: The two authors—Brad M. Barber, a professor at the University of California at Davis, and Terrance Odean, a professor at the University of California at Berkeley—show that individual investors are net buyers of attention-grabbing stocks. Given the "search problem"— the challenge of selecting stocks for purchase from the universe of available stocks—this finding is not surprising. However, the authors provide empirical evidence that attention-grabbing stocks—stocks that are in the news or that experience abnormal one-day returns or trading volumes—subsequently do not perform as well as stocks the same investors decided to sell. Barber and Odean base their study on data from four sources: a large discount brokerage, a small discount brokerage, a large full-service brokerage, and the Plexus Group, a consulting group that tracks the trading of professional money managers for institutional clients. Data from the Plexus Group demonstrate that attention-grabbing events are less likely to influence the buying decisions of professional investors, particularly those who employ the value style of investing. The authors recommend that retail investors buy and hold a well-diversified portfolio. The paper has seven sections: (1) "Related Research," (2) "Data," (3) "Sort Methodology," (4) "Results," (5) "Short-Sale Constraints," (6) "Conclusion," and (7) "Appendix: The Model."

Barber, Brad M., and Terrance Odean. "Boys Will Be Boys: Gender, Overconfidence, and Common Stock Investment." *Quarterly Journal of Economics* 116, no. 1 (February 2001): 261–92. Available by subscription: http://www.jstor.org/stable/2696449 (accessed December 10, 2009). Also available: http://faculty.gsm.ucdavis.edu/~bmbarber/ Paper%20Folder/QJE%20BoysWillBeBoys.pdf (accessed January 15, 2010).

Abstract: Barber, a professor at the University of California at Davis, and Odean, a professor at the University of California at Berkeley, explore the possibility of a correlation between investors' gender and their involvement in frequent trading. Based on the analysis of a large discount brokerage's account data for more than 35,000 households, from February 1991 to January 1997, the authors find that men trade 45 percent more often than women trade. Furthermore, "trading reduces men's net returns by 2.65 percentage points a year as opposed to 1.72 percentage points for women." The authors attribute this difference in gender behavior to male overconfidence. The correlation between male overconfidence and excessive trading is even more apparent when comparing single men and single women. The paper has five sections: (1) "A Test of Overconfidence," (2) "Data and Methods," (3) "Results," (4) "Competing Explanations for Differences in Turnover and Performance," and (5) "Conclusion."

Barber, Brad M., and Terrance Odean. "The Courage of Misguided Convictions." *Financial Analysts Journal* 55, no. 6 (November–December 1999): 41–55. Available by subscription: *http://www.jstor.org/stable/4480208* (accessed December 10, 2009). Also available: http://faculty.haas.berkeley.edu/odean/Papers%20current%20versions/ FAJ% 20NovDec99%20Barber%20and%20Odean.pdf (accessed January 15, 2010).

Abstract: University of California professors Barber and Odean provide an accessible introduction to behavioral finance, which offers an alternative to financial economic theory positing that investors behave with extreme rationality. The authors demonstrate how behavioral finance incorporates "observable, systematic, and very human departures into standard models of financial markets," highlighting two common investor mistakes: excessive trading and the disposition effect. The disposition effect is the tendency of investors to sell winning positions and to hold onto losing positions. Barber and Odean link these common behaviors to human psychology—to overconfidence, in the case of excessive trading, and to "the human desire to avoid regret," in the case of the disposition effect. They base their analysis on the trading activity of 10,000 randomly selected accounts from a national discount brokerage, covering January 1987 to December 1993. The paper has four sections: (1) "The Data," (2) "The Disposition Effect," (3) "Overconfidence and Excessive Trading," and (4) "Conclusion."

Barber, Brad M., and Terrance Odean. "Online Investors: Do the Slow Die First?" *Review of Financial Studies* 15, no. 2 (2002): 455–87. Available by subscription: http://www.jstor. org/stable/2696785 (accessed December 10, 2009). Also available: http://faculty.haas. berkeley.edu/odean/Papers% 20current%20versions/Online%20RFS.pdf (accessed January 15, 2010).

Abstract: University of California professors Barber and Odean investigate whether online traders achieve better results than investors who use traditional brokers and remain in touch with their brokers by telephone. Barber and Odean base their research on 1,607 investors who switched from telephone trading to online trading during the 1990s. They find that these investors' performance actually deteriorated—from beating the market by more than 2 percent annually to lagging behind the market by more than 3 percent annually. The authors attribute this outcome to overconfidence, which led the investors to trade more actively and speculatively, damaging their performance in the process. Overconfidence involves self-attribution bias, in which an individual ascribes his or her successes to personal abilities and his or her failures to bad luck or to the actions of others, as well as the illusion of knowledge and the illusion of control. In response to the question that they pose in the title of their article—"Online Investors: Do the Slow Die First?"—the authors conclude that a slow-trading, buy-and-hold strategy is actually superior to rapid, "trigger-happy" trading. The paper has seven sections: (1) "A Test of Overconfidence," (2) "Data and Methods," (3) "Who Goes Online?" (4) "Results," (5) "Discussion," (6) "Conclusion," and (7) appendices ("Appendix A: The Analysis of Time Trading" and "Appendix B: The Analysis of Intramonth Trades").

Barber, Brad M., and Terrance Odean. "Trading is Hazardous to Your Wealth: The Common Stock Investment Performance of Individual Investors." *Journal of Finance* 55, no. 2 (April 2000): 773–806. Available by subscription: http://www.jstor.org/stable/222522 (December 10, 2009). Also available: http://faculty.haas.berkeley.edu/odean/Papers% 20current%20 versions/Individual _Investor _Performance _Final.pdf (accessed January 15, 2010).

Abstract: Barber and Odean, professors at the University of California, demonstrate the pitfalls of active trading. By analyzing the discount brokerage accounts of 66,465 households that invested in common stocks from 1991 to 1996, Barber and Odean find that active traders earned an average return of 11.4 percent, well below the market return of 17.9 percent. On average, investors in common stock tend to favor high-beta (volatile), small, value stocks and turned over 75 percent of their portfolios annually, incurring high trading costs. The authors attribute investors' excessive trading and their subpar results to overconfidence. Incidentally, they find that investors act in a manner contrary to price momentum, retaining investments that have recently underperformed and selling winners. The paper has seven sections: (1) "Related Research," (2) "Data and Methods," (3) "Results," (4) "Overconfidence and Performance," (5) "Price Momentum," (6) "Liquidity, Rebalancing, and Tax-Motivated Trading," and (7) "Conclusion."

Barberis, Nicholas, Andrei Shleifer, and Robert Vishny. "A Model of Investor Sentiment." *Journal of Financial Economics* 49, 3 (September 1, 1998): 307–43. Available by subscription: http://www.sciencedirect.com/ (accessed January 16, 2010). Also available: http://www.lingnan.org/cferm/files/amodelofinvestorsentiment.pdf (accessed January 5, 2010) and http://www.lsvasset.com/pdf/Investor-Sentiment.pdf (accessed January 15, 2010).

Abstract: When Nicholas Barberis and Robert Vishny wrote this article, they were professors at the University of Chicago's Graduate School of Business; Andrei Shleifer was a professor of economics at Harvard University. The authors present a "parsimonious model," suggesting that investor sentiment (how investors form expectations of future earnings) is associated with the underreaction of stock prices to short-term news, such as earnings announcements, and with the overreaction of stock prices to a series of announcements of good or bad news. The authors call their model "parsimonious" because it involves one investor and one asset. "Conservatism" (the slowness to change beliefs in the face of new evidence) may explain underreaction, and the "representativeness heuristic" (the tendency to see patterns in truly random sequences) may explain overreaction. The finding of the parsimonious model is at odds with the efficient market hypothesis (EMH). The paper has seven sections: (1) "Introduction," (2) "The Evidence," (3) "Some Psychological Evidence," (4) "A Model of Investor

Sentiment," (5) "Model Solution and Empirical Implications," (6) "Conclusion," and (7) "Appendix."

Barberis, Nicholas, Ming Huang, and Tano Santos. "Prospect Theory and Asset Prices." *The Quarterly Journal of Economics* 116, no. 1 (February 2001): 1–53. http://badger.som. yale.edu/faculty/ncb25/bhs_jnl.pdf (accessed May 18, 2010).

Abstract: Nicholas Barberis is a finance professor at Yale University, Ming Huang is a finance professor at Cornell University, and Tano Santos is a finance and business professor at Columbia University. Their thesis is that investors "derive direct utility not only from consumption but also from fluctuations in the value of their personal wealth." Therefore, when deciding how much to invest in the stock market, investors take into account not just consumption growth, but also the performance of their stock portfolios. Since investors are loss-averse, prior losses in their portfolios lead them to be reluctant to invest out of fear of incurring additional losses. On the other hand, they view gains as a cushion that enables them to take on risk. In general, investors demand a high equity risk premium to compensate them for the risks of holding stocks. In a model of the economy consisting of a single asset, the authors find that consistent with historical data, "stock returns have a high mean, are excessively volatile, and are significantly predictable in a time series." The paper has seven sections: 1) "Introduction," 2) "Investor Preferences," 3) "Evidence from Psychology," 4) "Equilibrium Prices," 5) "Numerical Results and Further Discussion," 6) "The Importance of Prior Outcomes," and 7) "Conclusion."

Barberis, Nicholas, and Wei Xiong. "What Drives the Disposition Effect? An Analysis of a Long-Standing Preference-Based Explanation." *Journal of Finance* 64, no. 2 (April 2009): 751–84. Available by subscription: www.interscience.wiley.com/ (accessed January 20, 2010). Also available: http://www.princeton.edu/~wxiong/papers/ disposition.pdf (accessed January 5, 2010).

Abstract: Nicholas Barberis, a finance professor at the Yale School of Management, and Wei Xiong, an economics professor at Princeton University, investigate whether prospect theory (how people maximize value or utility functions when choosing between alternatives that involve risk) can predict a disposition effect (investors' propensity to sell winning positions and to retain losing positions). The authors find, to their surprise, that the annual gain/loss model of prospect theory (including gains and/or losses on paper, rather than only those realized through actual sales) often fails to predict a disposition effect, whereas the realized gain/loss model of prospect theory predicts this effect more reliably. Therefore, they suggest that utility from realized gains and losses may provide insight into the trading activity of individual investors. The paper has six sections: (1) "The Disposition Effect: Evidence and Interpretation," (2) "A Model that Applies Prospect Theory to Annual Trading Profits," (3) "A Model that Applies Prospect Theory to Realized Gains and Losses," (4) "Related Research and Other Applications," (5) "Conclusion," and (6) "Appendix."

Benartzi, Shlomo, and Richard H. Thaler. "Myopic Loss Aversion and the Equity Risk Premium." *Quarterly Journal of Economics* 110, no. 1 (February 1995): 73–92. Available by subscription: http://www.jstor.org/stable/2118511 (accessed December 10, 2009).

Abstract: UCLA business school professor Shlomo Benartzi and Richard H. Thaler, a business school professor at the University of Chicago, are pioneers in the field of behavioral finance. In this article discussing the phenomenon of the equity risk premium—stocks' substantial outperformance of bonds over the previous half century—the authors offer a new explanation for the allocation of stocks and bonds in portfolios. They draw on two behavioral finance concepts—loss aversion and the tendency of even long-term investors to evaluate their portfolios frequently—calling the combination of these two propensities "myopic loss aversion." Using simulations, Benartzi and Thaler find that the equity risk premium is consistent with prospect theory. According to prospect theory, investors seek to maximize prospective utility (gains). The authors attempt to extend their argument, applying this explanation, not only to individuals, but also to pension funds and to foundation and university endowments. The paper has seven sections: (1) "Introduction," (2) "Is the Equity Premium Real?" (3) "Prospect Theory and Loss Aversion," (4) "How Often are Portfolios Evaluated?" (5) "Myopia and the Magnitude of the Equity Premium," (6) "Do Organizations Display Myopic Loss Aversion?" and (7) "Conclusions."

Benartzi, Shlomo, and Richard H. Thaler. "Risk Aversion or Myopia? Choices in Repeated Gambles and Retirement Investments." *Management Science* 45, no. 3 (March 1999): 364–81. Available from several vendors by subscription, including: http://www.jstor.org/stable/2634883 (accessed December 10, 2009).

Abstract: This is Benartzi and Thaler's second paper on myopic loss aversion—the sensitivity to loss in a single trial, versus multiple plays of the same gamble (see the abstract for Benartzi and Thaler's article, "Myopic Loss Aversion and the Equity Risk Premium"). Exploring a preliminary finding that the economist Paul Samuelson articulated in 1963, the authors find that gamblers are more willing to accept the risk associated with repeated bets, versus a single bet, if they understand that the chances of a positive return over time are favorable. Next, they demonstrate that the same principle applies to asset allocation in pension plans. Specifically, Benartzi and Thaler find that, if investors understand the superior long-term returns of stocks, they are more likely to invest in them. The authors recommend that pension plans provide greater disclosure of long-term expected returns, to discourage investors from engaging in "narrow framing," such as "thinking about gambles or investments one at a time rather than aggregating them into a portfolio." The authors base their analysis on data regarding the investment behavior of faculty at the University of Southern California and the University of California. The paper has seven sections: (1) "Introduction," (2) "Literature Review," (3) "Samuelson's Bet (Study 1)," (4) "Preferences for Repeated Gambles (Study 2)," (5) "Preferences for Repeated Investments (Study 3)," (6) "Retirement Investing Sensitivity Analysis (Study 4)," and (7) "Conclusions."

Hirshleifer, David, and Siew Hong Teoh. "Herd Behavior and Cascading in Capital Markets: A Review and Synthesis."*European Financial Management* 9, no. 1 (March 2003): 25–66. Available by subscription: http://search.ebscohost.com/ (accessed January 20, 2010) and http://www.interscience.wiley.com/ (accessed January 20, 2010). Also available: http://www.blackwell-synergy.com/doi/abs/10.1111/1468-036X.00207 (accessed January 25, 2010).

Abstract: David Hirshleifer and Siew Hong Teoh, affiliated with Ohio State University when they published this article, investigate study participants' social learning (observing others); herd behavior (converging); payoff and reputational interactions (taking into account mutual impact among parties); and informational cascades (basing decisions about how to act on observations of others, rather than relying on one's own information signals). Study participants include investors and others with a stake in capital markets, such as analysts and companies. Hirschleifer and Teoh examine alternative theories for these practices, as well as incentives to engage in these behaviors and to exploit the tendency of others to do so. This research explores influences neglected by theorists who posit rational investment behavior—for example, the impact of noise (spurious signals)—to provide valuable insights into capital market behavior. The authors do not perform any data analysis of their own but instead review other academic research. The paper has nine sections: (1) "Introduction," (2) "Taxonomy and Mechanisms of Social Learning and Behavioural Convergence," (3) "Basic Principles and Alternative Economic Scenarios in Rational Learning Models," (4) "Agency/Reputation-Based Herding Models," (5) "Herd Behaviour and Cascades in the Analysis of Securities," (6) "Herd Behaviour and Cascades in Security Trading," (7) "Herding, Bubbles, and Crashes: The Price Implications of Herding and Cascading," (8) "Herd Behaviour and Cascades in Firms' Investment, Financing, and Reporting Decisions," and (9) "Conclusion."

Hong, Harrison, and Jeremy C. Stein. "A Unified Theory of Underreaction, Momentum Trading, and Overreaction in Asset Markets." *Journal of Finance* 54, no. 6 (December 1999): 2143–84. http://www.economicsharvard.edu/faculty/stein/files/UnifiedTheory.pdf (accessed May 20, 2010).

Abstract: At the time this article was written, Harrison Hong and Jeremy Stein were business school professors at Stanford and MIT, respectively. The article is noteworthy because it highlights the behavioral theories of short-run momentum and long-run reversals. Momentum means the continuation of a price trend, which, the authors maintain, may hold over the short or medium term until stock prices tend to overshoot the intrinsic value of the shares, leading to a long-term reversal. Although the authors are interested in such stock price performance, the focus here will be on investor behavior. Specifically, the authors develop a model that features two types of agents, "newswatchers" and "momentum traders," both of which are subject to bounded rationality in the sense of not taking into account all available public information. Newswatchers pay attention to some privately observed information but disregard current or past prices. Momentum traders do pay attention to current or past prices, but they base their forecasts on simple, univariate functions of price history, disregarding other information. If the information observed by newswatchers spreads slowly, prices may underreact, causing momentum traders, who attempt to capitalize on trends, to step in.

This in turns leads to a price overreaction, followed by a reversal. Slow information diffusion is characteristic of small-cap stocks with low analyst coverage. The paper has seven sections: 1) "Evidence of Continuations and Reversals," 2) "The Model," 3) "Extensions of the Basic Model: More Rational Arbitrage," 4) "Empirical Implications," 5) "Comparison to Related Work," 6) "Conclusions," and appendices ("Appendix A: Proofs" and "Appendix B: Numerical Comparative Statics").

Huberman, Gur. "Familiarity Breeds Investment." *Review of Financial Studies* 14, no. 3 (Autumn 2001): 659–80. Available by subscription: http://www.jstor.org/stable/2696769 (accessed December 10, 2009).

Abstract: Gur Huberman, a professor of behavioral finance at Columbia University's Graduate School of Business, investigates the geographic bias in investing, studying individuals in the seven Regional Bell Operating Companies (RBOCs). Huberman finds that "in every state but Montana, more people hold shares of the local RBOC than of any other single RBOC. In most states, more money is invested, per investor, in the local RBOC than in any other RBOC." Huberman's finding is consistent with many examples illustrating the tendency to invest in the familiar—in one's own country, region, state, and company. Nonetheless, such a practice violates the principle of diversification set out in portfolio theory, which emphasizes the financial attributes of investments. The paper has four sections: (1) "Instances of Investment in the Familiar," (2) "Evidence on the Regional Bell Operating Companies," (3) "Decision Theory and Investment in the Familiar," and (4) "Concluding Remarks."

Ivković, Zoran, Clemens Sialm, and Scott Weisbenner. "Portfolio Concentration and the Performance of Individual Investors." *Journal of Financial and Quantitative Analysis* 43, no. 3 (September 2008): 613–56. Available by subscription: http://search.ebscohost.com/ (accessed January 5, 2010).

Abstract: Zoran Ivković, Clemens Sialm, and Scott Weisbenner are finance professors at Michigan State University, the University of Texas at Austin, and the University of Illinois at Urbana-Champaign, respectively. The authors find that, contrary to conventional financial advice to invest in well-diversified portfolios, some individual investors (particularly from households with large portfolios) achieve superior returns by concentrating their investments in a few stocks, notwithstanding investment ability. Excess returns correlate with local stocks, stocks not included in the S&P 500 index (small capitalization stocks), and stocks with less analyst coverage. Using data on the investments that 78,000 households made through a discount broker, from January 1991 to November 1996, (data from trades and monthly position statements), the authors investigate, and ultimately reject the hypothesis that the success of these investors is attributable to information advantages or asymmetries. The authors conclude that "results are not driven by specialization in a particular industry, inside information, broad market timing, repeated trades in a particular stock, or regional difference across investors. Rather, the results seem to reflect that wealthy households who concentrate their holdings in a few stocks tend to have the ability to identify superior stock picks." The paper has seven sections: (1) "Introduction," (2) "Data and Summary Statistics," (3) "Performance of Holdings," (4) "Performance of Trades," (5) "Robustness Tests," (6) "Risk-Return Trade-Off for Concentrated Investors," and (7) "Conclusion."

Odean, Terrance. "Are Investors Reluctant to Realize Their Losses?" *Journal of Finance* 53, no. 5 (October 1998): 1775–98. Available by subscription: http://www.jstor.org/stable/ 117424 (accessed December 10, 2009). Also available: http://faculty.haas.berkeley.edu/odean/Papers%20current%20versions/AreInvestorsReluctant.pdf (accessed January 15, 2010).

Abstract: Odean bases this article on his PhD dissertation, defended at the University of California at Berkeley, where he is currently a professor of banking and finance at the Haas School of Business. Analyzing discount brokerage trading records for 10,000 accounts, from 1987 to 1993, Odean confirms the disposition effect: "the tendency of investors to hold losing investments too long and sell winning investments too soon." He finds that investors demonstrate a strong tendency to realize gains on winning investments, while holding onto losing investments, possibly in the hope of recouping their losses. However, in the months following the sale of the winning investments, these investments continue to outperform the losing ones still held in the investment portfolio. Furthermore, investors lose the benefits of tax-loss selling. Odean concludes that investor behavior is consistent with prospect theory—the theory that holds that people maximize value or utility functions. In the case of investing, these value or utility functions represent gains. The paper has five sections: (1) "The Disposition Effect," (2) "The Data Set," (3) "Empirical Study," (4) "Discussion," and (5) "Conclusion."

Efficient Market Hypothesis

Malkiel, Burton G. "The Efficient Market Hypothesis and Its Critics." *Journal of Economic Perspectives* 17, no. 1 (Winter 2003): 59–82. Available by subscription: http://www.jstor.org/stable/32 16840 (accessed December 10, 2009). Also available: http://www.princeton. edu/~ceps/workingpapers/9 1 malkiel.pdf (accessed January 15, 2010).

Abstract: Burton G. Malkiel, a professor of economics at Princeton University, is associated with the random-walk theory of investing. This theory, which holds that in a price series for securities all "subsequent price changes represent random departures from previous prices," is consistent with the efficient market hypothesis (EMH), which financial economists have widely accepted since 1970, when University of Chicago economist Eugene Fama wrote an article on this topic. In this article, Malkiel attempts to rebut recent EMH critics who emphasize the "psychological and behavioral elements of stock-price determination." Malkiel concludes, "our stock markets are far more efficient and far less predictable than some recent academic papers would have us believe. Moreover, the evidence is overwhelming that whatever anomalous behavior of stock prices exist, it does not create a portfolio trading opportunity that enables investors to earn extraordinary risk adjusted returns."

Malkiel discusses and rejects various theories favored by behavioral economists, specifically, as follows:

- Short-term momentum, including underreaction to new information (behavioral economists relate this supposed phenomenon to psychological feedback mechanisms)
- Long-run return reversals (some behavioral economists recommend contrarian investing)
- Seasonal and day-of-the-week patterns
- Predictable patterns based on valuation parameters (such as initial dividend yields and initial price-earnings multiples)
- Cross-sectional predictable patterns, based on firm characteristics and valuation parameters (the size effect, value stocks, and the equity risk premium puzzle—stocks outperforming bonds over the long term)

Malkiel also addresses specific events that critics of market efficiency often highlight, including the market crash of October 1987 and the Internet bubble of the late 1990s. Finally, as evidence supporting the EMH, he points to index funds' outperformance of actively managed funds. The article is divided into six sections: (1) "A Nonrandom Walk Down Wall Street," (3) "Predictable Patterns Based on Valuation Parameters," (4) "Cross-Sectional Predictable Patterns Based on Firm Characteristics and Valuation Parameters," (5) "Seemingly Irrefutable Cases of Inefficiency," (6) "The Performance of Professional Investors," and (7) "Conclusion."

Institutional Investing

Bennett, James A., Richard W. Sias, and Laura T. Starks. "Greener Pastures and the Impact of Dynamic Institutional Preferences." *Review of Financial Studies* 16, no. 4 (Winter 2003): 1203–38. Available by subscription: http://www.jstor.org/stable/1262741 (accessed December 10, 2009).

Abstract: Authors James A. Bennet of the University of Massachusetts, Richard W. Sias of Washington State University, and Laura T. Starks of the University of Texas find that, although institutional investors generally prefer large-capitalization stocks, during the past 10 years, they have become increasingly willing to hold smaller, riskier stocks. The authors attribute 93 percent of this shift to investor preferences and the remainder to changes in the profile (types) of institutional investors. Furthermore, they maintain that this shift has led to a relative increase in smaller stocks' liquidity and in firm-specific risk. The authors identify two reasons for the shift: (1) institutions' historical preference for large-cap stocks has driven up the stocks' valuations, leading to lower book-to-market ratios, and investors view small-cap stocks as less expensive; and (2) institutional investors are better able to exploit informational advantages with small-cap stocks. Both of these reasons are consistent with the hypothesis that institutional investors believe that small-cap stocks offer "greener pastures." The paper has six sections: (1) "Data," (2) "Changes in Institutional Preferences over Time," (3) "Understanding Changes in Aggregate Institutional Preferences," (4) "The Impact on Turnover and Volatility," (5) "Why the Shift in Institutional Preferences?" and (6) "Conclusion."

Binay, Murat. "Performance Attribution of U.S. Institutional Investors." *Financial Management* 34, no. 2 (Summer 2005): 127–52. Available by subscription: http://www.jstor.org/stable/3666353 (accessed January 5, 2010).

Abstract: Murat Binay, a professor of finance at Claremont Graduate School, evaluates the performance of institutional investors in the management of client assets. Using factor-model regression, he concludes that investors add "significant value by generating excess returns after controlling for underlying portfolio risk factors." Superior performance is attributable, primarily, to the choice of investment style and, secondarily, to skill in stock selection. The author defines institutional investors as "fiduciary entit[ies] established to manage client assets with full investment discretion." They include banks and bank trust departments; insurance companies; investment advisors; investment companies (mutual fund families); and endowments, philanthropic foundations, and public and corporate pension funds. The author used data from an SEC filing database of 13F reports filed from 1981 through 2002, by institutional investors managing portfolios worth at least $100 million. The paper has seven sections: (1) "Data," (2) "Background on the Institutional Investor Universe," (3) "Factor Model Portfolio Performance Evaluation," (4) "Performance Decomposition: Stock Selection, Investment Timing, and Investment Style," (5) "Taxes, Fees, and Transaction Costs," (6) "Conclusion," and (7) appendices ("Appendix A: 13F Institutional Shareholdings Database" and "Appendix B: Construction of the Characteristic-Based Benchmark Portfolios").

Garvey, Ryan, and Anthony Murphy. "Are Professional Traders Too Slow to Realize Their Losses?" *Financial Analysts Journal* 60, no. 4 (July–August 2004): 35–43. Available by subscription: http://www.jstor.org/stable/4480586 (accessed December 10, 2009).

Abstract: Ryan Garvey, a professor of finance at Duquesne University in Pittsburgh, and Anthony Murphy, a senior lecturer in economics at University College Dublin, Ireland, examine the disposition effect—the tendency of investors to sell winning positions and to hold onto losing positions—as it applies to proprietary traders. The authors claim that their article is the first to examine proprietary traders, in contrast to previous research by Terrance Odean and others, regarding the disposition effect in the world of retail investing. By analyzing the activities, from March 8 to June 13, 2000, of 15 professional stock traders working for a U.S. direct-access broker, Garvey and

Murphy find evidence of the disposition effect. The authors conclude, "This tendency lowered their profitability. When the traders limited their risk exposure by trading in small share sizes, in low-priced stocks, or during periods of low volatility, the discrepancy between losing and winning holding times rose. An analysis of intraday prices suggests that traders could increase trading profits by holding winners longer and selling losers sooner." The authors attribute the distribution effect to two factors: "the human tendency to seek pride and avoid regret" and self-control measures in the form of stop-loss orders. The paper has four sections: (1) "The Disposition Effect," (2) "Data and Methodology," (3) "Empirical Results," and (4) "Are Holding Times Justified?"

Investing Styles

Chan, Louis K., Hsiu-Lang Chen, and Josef Lakonishok. "On Mutual Fund Investment Styles." *Review of Financial Studies* 15, no. 5 (Winter 2002): 1407–37. Available by subscription: http://www.jstor.org/stable/1262659 (accessed December 10, 2009).

Abstract: Louis K. Chan, Hsiu-Lang Chen, and Josef Lakonishok, all affiliated with the University of Illinois, analyze the impact of investment style (growth, income, or balanced styles) on mutual fund performance. Although extreme departures from the benchmark index are rare, some evidence indicates that portfolio managers favor growth stocks, glamour stocks, and past winners. The authors find that, although value stocks generally outperform growth stocks, "few funds consistently generate superior performance." The same holds for the performance of pension funds. According to one explanation for this trend, incentives for mutual fund and pension fund managers may involve considerations other than the maximization of portfolio return or diversification. Other possible factors include agency and behavioral considerations, such as concern about career risk, herding behavior, and hubris. The authors also find that, "after adjusting for style, there is evidence that growth managers on average outperform value managers." Finally, the authors believe that examining such factors as size and the book-tomarket ratio (the balance-sheet-carrying value of a security, relative to its market value) can help provide a useful description of fund styles. The paper has seven sections: (1) "Mutual Fund Investment Styles," (2) "Mutual Fund Portfolio Characteristics," (3) "Mutual Fund Factor Exposures,"

(4) "Fund Style and Fund Performance," (5) "Shifts in Fund Style," (6) "Comparing Approaches to Style Measurement," and (7) "Conclusion."

Chan, Louis K. C. and Josef Lakonishok. "Value and Growth Investing: Review and Update." *Financial Analysts Journal*, 60, no. 1 (January–February 2004): 7 1–86. Available by subscription: http://www.jstor.org/stable/4480542 (accessed January 12, 2010). Also available: http://www.lsvasset.com/pdf/Value-Review.pdf (accessed January 26, 2010).

Abstract: Louis Chan and Josef Lakonishok are finance professors at the University of Illinois at Urbana-Champaign. The authors maintain that value investing generates superior returns to growth investing, particularly for small-capitalization stocks. The value style of investing entails buying out-of-favor stocks with low price-to-earnings and price-to-book value ratios and therefore believed to be trading below their intrinsic value. Growth style of investing is an approach to investing that focuses on high-growth stocks even if they have high price-to-earning ratios. The authors' assertion comes with a significant caveat: the superior performance of value stocks held prior to 1990, but this trend was reversed during the 1990s. The authors attribute this reversal to excessive enthusiasm during that decade for technology, media, and telecom stocks that defied economic logic. The authors attribute the pre-1990 return differential of value over growth stocks to behavioral considerations and the "agency costs of delegated investment management" rather than the higher riskiness of value stocks. Behavioral considerations include the extrapolation of past performance too far into the future. Although growth rates tend not to persist, investors may underestimate the ability of value stocks to improve their performance and overestimate the ability of glamour stocks to maintain above-average growth. Agency costs of delegating investment decisions to professionals involve the tendency of analysts, money managers, and pension plan executives to promote or invest in glamour stocks. Reasons include investment banking-related conflicts of interests by analysts, career concerns of money managers, and excitement about emerging technologies. Whether behavioral or agency factors are in play, the prices of growth stocks may be driven up beyond their fundamental values. Such mispricing may persist for a long time but not indefinitely, while unappreciated value stocks eventually recover. In other words, growth stocks fail to meet optimistic expectations while value stocks exceed pessimistic expectations. The paper has five sections: (1) "Introduction," (2) "Returns on value investing," (3) "Explaining the performance of value strategies," (4) "Evidence updated," and (5) "Conclusion."

Investment Clienteles

Agnew, Julie R., Lisa R. Anderson, Jeffrey R. Gerlach, and Lisa R. Szykman. "Who Chooses Annuities? An Experimental Investigation of the Role of Gender, Framing and Defaults." *American Economic Review* 98, no. 2 (May 2008): 418–22. http://lrande.people.wm. edu/links/AERP&P&P2008.pdf (accessed May 13, 2010).

Abstract: Professors Julie Agnew, Lisa Anderson, and Lisa Szykman of the College of William and Mary and Jeffrey Gerlach of the Massachusetts Institute of Technology build on past research into gender differences with respect to risk aversion and financial literacy. In this study, they examine how women and men differ in how they approach the decision between purchasing an annuity and investing on their own. Even controlling for risk aversion and financial literacy, they still find that women are more likely than men to purchase an annuity. The experiment involves a framing technique whereby participants are shown slide shows highlighting the positive or negative aspects of annuity investing or presenting a neutral point of view. Women are more likely than men to be dissuaded from buying annuities after seeing the negative presentation. This raises the issue that financial advisors may inadvertently influence investment decisions by how they present options. The article has six sections: 1) "Why the Annuity Decision?" 2) "Why Might Gender Matter?" 3) "Defaults and Framing," 4) "Experimental Design," 5) "The Results," and 6) "Discussion."

Graham, John R., and Alok Kumar. "Do Dividend Clienteles Exist? Evidence on Dividend Preferences of Retail Investors." *Journal of Finance* 61, no. 3 (June 2006): 1305–36. Available by subscription: http://web. ebscohost.com/ (accessed January 5, 2010).

Abstract: Business professors John R. Graham of Duke University and Alok Kumar of the University of Notre Dame analyze data from more than 60,000 retail investor accounts at a large U.S. discount brokerage during the period 199 1–96. The authors find that older and lower- income investors favor stocks with high dividend yields, and that, in their investment timing, these investors take into account dividend announcements and ex-dividend dates. The investors also make an effort to offset the impact of taxes by holding high-dividend stocks in tax-deferred accounts. This research provides valuable evidence regarding dividend clienteles, in contrast to clienteles who favor capital gains. The paper has five sections: (1) "Data and Sample Characteristics," (2) "Dividend Preferences of Retail Investors and Dividend Clienteles," (3) Trading Behavior around Dividend Events," (4) "Summary and Conclusion," and (5) "Appendix: Dividend Preference Measures."

Limited Stock-Market Participation

Guiso, Luigi, Paola Sapienza, and Luigi Zingales. "Trusting the Stock Market." *Journal of Finance* 63, no. 6 (December 2008): 2557–2600. http://www.bus.wisc.edu/finance/Meyferth/Fedenia/Articles/Guiso%20Sapienza%20Zingales%202007.pdf (accessed May 19, 2010).

Abstract: Luigi Guiso, Paola Sapienza, and Luigi Zingales are affiliated with the European University Institute, Northwestern University, and the University of Chicago, respectively. They attribute limited participation in the stock market to a lack of trust and the fear of being cheated, particularly among wealthy investors. Subjective and cultural factors play a role in how trusting people are and therefore whether and how much they are willing to invest. The authors maintain that trust is not a proxy for risk tolerance. It should be noted that the study involves a mathematical model using Dutch and Italian micro data, although cross-country data include the United States. The paper has eight sections: 1) "The Model," 2) "The Main Data," 3) "Results," 4) "Is Trust a Proxy for Risk Tolerance?" 5) "Is Generalized or Personalized Trust that Matters?" 6) "The Effect of Trust on Stock Market Participation across Countries," 7) "Conclusions," and 8) appendices ("Appendix A," "Appendix B: the DNB Survey and the Bank Customers Survey," and "Appendix C: Measuring Risk and Ambiguity Aversion").

Van Rooij, Maarten, Annamaria Lusardi, and Rob Alessie. "Financial Literacy and Stock Market Participation." National Bureau of Economic Research Working Paper 13565, October 2007. http://www.nber.org/papers/w13565 (accessed May 21, 2010).

Abstract: Maarten van Rooij is affiliated with the Dutch Central Bank, Rob Alessie is an economics professor at Utrecht University, and Annamaria Lusardi is an economics professor at Dartmouth College. Based on questionnaires on financial literacy submitted to a sample of the Dutch population, the authors conclude that while most households are knowledgeable about basic financial concepts, such as compound interest, inflation, and the time value of money, very few households understand more advanced financial concepts often considered necessary for successful investing, such as the difference between stocks and bonds, the inverse relationship of bond prices and interest rates, and risk diversification. They find that those with low levels of financial literacy are less likely to invest in stocks. In fact, they establish a causal relationship, not just a correlation, so that the lack of financial literacy prevents stock-market participation. The reliance of this study on Dutch data does not invalidate it. In fact, in 2005 Lusardi and Olivia Mitchell found a widespread financial illiteracy among Americans, particularly women, the elderly, and the poorly educated (see the abstract of their article on "Financial Literacy and Planning: Implications for Retirement Wellbeing" in the section on Retirement Saving Adequacy). However, the authors of the Dutch study maintain that their questions are more extensive and that their results have been subject to more rigorous analysis, including changes in knowledge over time and controls for cognitive ability. The authors recommend that financial education programs designed for private retirement plans target the least financially sophisticated segments of the population in order to address their reluctance to invest in the stock market. The paper has seven sections: 1) "Introduction," 2) "Literature Review," 3) "Data," 4) "The Measurement of Literacy," 5) "Financial Literacy and Stock Market Participation," 6) "Discussion and Extensions," and 7) "Concluding Remarks."

Manias and Panics

Visano, Brenda Spotton. "Financial Manias and Panics: A Socioeconomic Perspective." *American Journal of Economics and Sociology* 61, no. 4 (October 2002): 801–27. Available by subscription: http://www.jstor.org/stable/3487980 (accessed January 5, 2010).

Abstract: Brenda Spotton Visano is an economics professor at York University in Toronto, Canada, but her analysis of the issue of financial manias and panics includes a strong sociological component. Visano does not provide any original research, but she uses her encyclopedic knowledge of sociological theory to illuminate the emergence of financial manias and panics. She argues that "the gradual diffusion of a revolutionary innovation" creates an environment of "optimistic uncertainty," consistent with the ideas of Nathan Rosenberg, an economist who specialized in the history of technology. German sociologist Georg Simmel's "theory of fashion" explains how this optimistic uncertainty turns into a "swell of speculative excitement." As economist Joseph Schumpeter observed, enthusiasm continues until the objective potential of the innovation becomes "apparent and estimable." If the optimism underpinning high prices turns out to be unfounded, a reversal of fortune results, leading to distress and possibly panic. In accordance with the theories of Kurt and Gladys Lang, sociologists who specialized in opinion research, objective market conditions—not necessarily a period of extreme speculation—can give rise to such panic. By combining economic and sociological analysis, the author sheds light on the development of speculative bubbles and collapses. The paper has 10 sections: (1) "Introduction," (2) "Economic Context, Related Perspectives, and Points of Departure," (3) "Revolutionary Innovation and Economic Sources of Instability," (4) "The Socioeconomics of Financial Manias and Panics," (5) "Preconditions: The Desire to Speculate," (6) "Proximate Causes and Precipitating Factors: The Opportunity to Speculate," (7) "The Speculation Process," (8) "Proximate Causes of Financial Panic: Peak and Distress," (9) "The Panic," and (10) "Summary and Conclusion."

Mutual Fund Disclosure

Beshears, John, James J. Choi, David Laibson, and Brigitte C. Madrian. "How Does Simplified Disclosure Affect Individuals' Mutual Fund Choices?" *National Bureau of Economic Research Working Paper* No. 14859 (March 27, 2009): 1–26, http://www.nber.org/papers/w14859 (accessed May 19, 2010).

Abstract: John Beshears is affiliated with the National Bureau of Economic Research, James Choi is a finance professor at Yale University, David Laibson is an economics professor at Harvard University, and Brigitte Madrian is public policy professor at Harvard University. The authors performed a portfolio allocation experiment to test the effectiveness of the Security and Exchange Commission's Summary Prospectus, which was introduced on January 13, 2009, as an alternative to the longer and more extensive conventional prospectus. The experiment, which was conducted with 186 Harvard non-faculty, white-collar staff, required them to select equity and bond funds based on different types of disclosure: the statutory prospectus, the Summary Prospectus, or the Summary Prospectus with the option to request the statutory version. The subjects were rewarded for the one-month or one-year performance of their portfolios. The results were that the Summary Prospectus did not alter the subjects' investment choices, but they used less time to reach the same decisions as the recipients of the statutory prospectus. Futhermore, the subjects disregarded the impact of loads on investment performance, even over the one-month time horizon. Therefore, the Summary Prospectus does not prevent this common investing mistake. The paper has five sections: 1) "Background on the Summary Prospectus," 2) "Experimental Design," 3) "Results," 4) "Conclusion," and 5) appendices ("Appendix A: The SEC's Sample Summary Prospectus (from Release No. 33-8861)," "Appendix B: Sample Experimental Investment Choice Sheet," and "Appendix C: Creating the Summary Prospectus").

Kozup, John, Elizabeth Howlett, and Michael Pagano. "The Effects of Summary Information on Consumer Perceptions of Mutual Fund Characteristics." *Journal of Consumer Affairs* 42, no. 1 (Spring 2008): 37–59. Available by subscription: http://proquest.umi.com/login (accessed December 10, 2009) and http://web.ebscohost.com/ (accessed January 22, 2010).

Abstract: Villanova University professors John Kozup, who teaches marketing, and Michael Pagano, who teaches finance, and Elizabeth Howlett, professor of marketing at the University of Arkansas, find that investors have trouble sifting through information about mutual fund characteristics. Moreover, prior fund performance, along with other extraneous factors, such as search costs (costs associated with selecting stocks for purchase from the universe of available stocks), the size of the mutual fund company, and the level of the company's marketing effort, tend to influence these investors unduly. Nevertheless, supplemental information disclosure, particularly in graphical format, helps investors make better choices, although they continue to place too much emphasis on prior fund performance. Investor education is important since, during the 10 years ending in 2002, company-managed investment accounts slightly outperformed employee-managed accounts, with median returns of 6.81 percent and 6.35 percent, respectively. Over a long-term investment horizon, such a seemingly minor disparity in the short term leads to a significant difference in outcome. The paper has six sections: (1)

"Background and Literature Review," (2) "Hypotheses," (3) "Method," (4) "Results," (5) "Discussion," and (6) appendices (1–4).

Wilcox, Ronald T. "Bargain Hunting or Star Gazing? Investors' Preferences for Stock Mutual Funds." *Journal of Business* 76, no. 4 (October 2003): 645–63. Available: http://faculty. darden.virginia.edu/wilcoxr/pdf_docs/BargainHuntingorStarGazing.pdf (accessed January 25, 2010).

Abstract: Ronald T. Wilcox, a professor at the University of Virginia, examines the criteria investors use to select stock mutual funds from among a class of funds. Analyzing the conjoint preferences (combinations of fund attributes) of 50 current mutual fund investors, he finds that "investors pay a great deal of attention to past performance and vastly overweight loads relative to expense ratios when evaluating a fund's overall fee structure." In other words, investors are much more concerned about the cost of buying a fund (load) than the cost of owning a fund (expense ratio). Taking into account the results of a 10-question quiz designed to determine the investors' knowledge of basic finance, Wilcox reaches the counter-intuitive conclusion that investors who are more knowledgeable tend to make less reasonable fund choices. Therefore, he recommends that investor education target the relatively sophisticated audiences who watch such programs as *Wall Street Week* and *Moneyline*. The paper has five sections: (1) "Introduction," (2) "A Conjoint Study of Mutual Fund Investors' Preferences," (3) "Managerial and Regulatory Implications," (4) "Limitations and Directions for Future Research," and (5) appendices (A, B, and C).

Neuroscience and Investing

Peterson, Richard L. "Affect and Financial Decision-Making: How Neuroscience Can Inform Market Participants." *Journal of Behavioral Finance* 8, no. 2 (2007): 70–78. Available by subscription: http://web. ebscohost.com/ (accessed January 5, 2010). Also available from the publisher for a fee.

Abstract: Richard L. Peterson, a medical doctor and a managing partner of Market Psychology Consulting, is the author of the book *Inside the Investor's Brain*, which Wiley published in 2007. Referring to recent literature in the field of neuroscience, Peterson identifies two separate brain systems linked to "affect processing" (the impact of emotions), which govern risk avoidance and risk taking in investing. The two systems comprise a "reward approach system," which transmits signals via the "pleasure chemical" dopamine, and a "loss avoidance system," which transmits signals via serotonin and norepinephrine. The author describes how various forms of mental illness, such as acute mania, depression, anxiety, and obsessive-compulsive behavior, accentuate the impact of emotions on investing. By educating investors about the potential adverse impact of emotions on their performance, he hopes they will be able to manage their emotions and make better investment decisions. Self-awareness and self-discipline can help investors avoid excessive market euphoria or fear. The paper has eight sections: (1) "Introduction," (2) "Reward and Loss Avoidance Systems in Decisions under Risk," (3) "Affect in Market Pricing," (4) "Emotions and Personality in the Trading Pit," (5) "Financial Decisions and Mental Health," (6) "The Neurochemistry of Risk Assessment, (7) "How to Make Better Financial Choices," and (8) "Conclusion."

Ponzi Schemes

Benson, Sandra S. "Recognizing the Red Flags of a Ponzi Scheme." *CPA Journal* 79, no. 6 (June 2009): 18–25. Available by subscription: http:// web.ebscohost.com/ (accessed January 22, 2010). Also available: http:// viewer.zmags.com/publication/95cbd4ae#/95cbd4ae/20 (accessed January 5, 2010).

Abstract: Sandra S. Benson is an attorney and a professor of business law at Middle Tennessee State University. Although financial auditors are the intended audience for this article, the author provides a readable and systematic overview of the characteristics of Ponzi schemes, including the case of Bernard Madoff. Particularly helpful for investors are sidebars explaining what happens to them when a Ponzi scheme collapses, enumerating 10 red flags that arose in the Madoff scheme, and suggesting how to identify and analyze the fraud risk factors for a Ponzi scheme. The author groups fraud risk factors according to incentive, opportunity, and attitude, and, for each of these, she specifies several possible warning signs. The paper has five sections: (1) "Wake-up Call," (2) "Ponzi Schemes Defined," (3) "Red Flags to Watch For," (4) "Should CPAs Detect a Ponzi Scheme from Red Flags?" and (5) "Reducing Liability Risk."

Pressman, Steven. "On Financial Frauds and Their Causes: Investor Overconfidence." *American Journal of Economics and Sociology* 57, no. 4 (October 1998): 405–21. Available by subscription: http://www.jstor.org/stable/3487115 (accessed December 10, 2009).

Abstract: Steven Pressman, an economics professor at Monmouth University in New Jersey, examines two possible explanations for why investors are taken in by financial scam artists and Ponzi schemers: the explanation that neoclassical economists propose, which assumes "asymmetric information in a world of calculable risk," and that of empirical psychologists, who explore "how people make choices in a world characterized by uncertainty." Pressman rejects the former explanation in favor of the latter. The author reviews the case study of New Era Philanthropy, a Ponzi scheme that John G. Bennett Jr. perpetrated from 1989 until 1995. In considering solutions to protect investors from such fraud, Pressman does not advocate providing more information about investments (disclosure), so that potential investors can make rational and intelligent decisions, but, instead, he favors providing more information about the risks of scams, "in concrete terms." He also recommends substantially increasing the penalties of such schemes, relative to rewards. Pressman concludes that "the best solution to the problem of financial fraud is to keep reminding investors about the Charles Ponzis, the Nick Leesons, the Crazy Eddies, and the John Bennetts." The paper has five sections: 1) "Introduction," (2) "New Era Philanthropy—A Case Study," (3) "The Causes of Financial Frauds—The Neoclassical Story," (4) "Causes of Financial Frauds—The Other Story," and (5) "Preventing Financial Frauds."

Portfolio Diversification

Statman, Meir. "The Diversification Puzzle." *Financial Analysts Journal* 60, no. 4 (July–August 2004): 44–53. Available by subscription: http://www.jstor.org/stable/4480587 (accessed January 5, 2010).

Abstract: Meir Statman, a professor of finance at Santa Clara University, explores the lack of diversification in U.S. investors' equity portfolios. Although mean-variance portfolio theory recommends that portfolios hold at least 300 stocks, the average investor actually holds only three or four, representing an extremely suboptimal portfolio. The typical investor's concentration in employer, large-capitalization, and domestic stocks exacerbates the vulnerability of portfolios with minimal diversification. Since mean-variance portfolio theory fails to predict that investors will choose minimal diversification, Statman offers an alternative explanation, which he called behavioral portfolio theory. According to this theory, investors are not always risk averse, nor do they consider their portfolios as a whole. In the most simplistic version, investors construct their portfolios as a two-layer pyramid, where the bottom layer provides protection against poverty and the upper layer is "designed to make them rich." In a more elaborate version, the pyramid consists of many layers, "each of which corresponds to a goal or aspiration." Therefore, according to Statman's theory, investors' aspirations, more than their attitudes toward risk, drive their behavior. The paper has three sections: (1) "Mean- Variance Diversification," (2) "Behavioral Diversification," and (3) "Conclusion."

Strong, Norman, and Xinzhong Xu. "Understanding the Equity Home Bias: Evidence from Survey Data." *Review of Economics and Statistics* 85, no. 2 (May 2003): 307–12. Available by subscription: http://www.jstor.org/stable/3211582 (accessed December 10, 2009).

Abstract: Norman Strong, of the University of Manchester in the United Kingdom, and Xinzhong Xu, affiliated with Peking University, investigate the equity home bias puzzle—why investors tend to favor their own country's equities, despite the advantages of international diversification. The authors base their research on data from the Merrill Lynch monthly *Fund Manager Survey*, which polls 250 large fund managers around the world about their views on markets, economics, and other issues. After reviewing relevant academic literature in the introduction, the authors explore behavioral explanations, including investors' relative optimism about the home market. However, the authors argue that this optimism alone cannot explain equity home bias. They consider the possibility that relative optimism is not the "driving force behind the domestic equity bias," but "an ex post justification for investing in domestic equities." In fact, fund sponsors who constrain fund managers or measure their performance against domestic benchmarks may drive them to invest in domestic equities. The paper has six sections: (1) "Introduction," (2) "Relative Optimism," (3) "The Merrill Lynch Fund Manager Survey," (4) "Do Fund Managers' Sentiments Display a Home Bias?" (5) "Are Expressions of Sentiment Consistent with Investment Intentions?" and (6) "Conclusion and Discussion."

Psychology and Investing

Mohacsy, Ildiko, and Heidi Lefer. "Money and Sentiment: A Psychodynamic Approach to Behavioral Finance." *Journal of the American Academy of Psychoanalysis and Dynamic Psychiatry* 35, no. 3 (fall 2007): 455–75. Available by subscription from a number of vendors including: http://proquest.umi.com/login (accessed January 13, 2010).

Abstract: Ildiko Mohacsy is a deceased medical doctor; Heidi Lefer is a member of the professional staff of the CUNY Research Foundation. Rejecting the efficient market hypothesis, the authors describe the stock market as a "conglomeration of human sentiment" (hope, fear, and greed) that is not subject to purely scientific analysis. Many investors engage in wishful or magical thinking rather than logical thinking, which leads to a series of destructive patterns described by behavioral finance. Most dangerous of all, many investors participate in herd and imitative behavior by blindly following the trend, an approach euphemistically called "momentum investing" but more accurately labeled as the Greater Fool Theory. The repeated occurrence of bubbles and busts—from Tulip Mania in Holland in 1634-3 8 and the South Sea Bubble in England in 1720 to the dot com bubble in the United States in 1998-2000—belies market efficiency. The authors point to the biological basis of financial speculation, particularly brain chemistry and the role of the neurotransmitter dopamine. This article is essentially an essay and does not present any original statistical analysis. The paper has 10 sections: (1) "Master of the mint," (2) "Markets and emotion," (3) "The maddening crowd," (4) "Bubble dynamics," (5) "Forever blowing bubbles," (6) "Mania and depression," (7) "Biology and speculation," (8) "Control," (9) "Fallibility of investment professionals," and (10) "Disdain."

Kahneman, Daniel, and Mark W. Riepe. "Aspects of Investor Psychology." *Journal of Portfolio Management* 24, no. 4 (Summer 1998): 52. http://corporate.morningstar.com/ib/documents/MethodologyDocuments/IBBAssociates/InvestorPsychology.pdf (accessed December 10, 2009).

Abstract: Daniel Kahneman is a professor of psychology at Princeton University and the winner of the Nobel Prize for Economics in 2002; Mark W. Riepe is an executive at Charles Schwab & Co. Scholars often cite Kahneman's work in the context of behavioral finance. The authors refer to the three types of analysis defined by decision theorist Howard Raiffa—normative, descriptive, and prescriptive analysis. They point out that financial advising is a form of prescriptive analysis, "concerned with practical advice and help that people could use to make more rational decisions." Therefore, the main objective of financial advising "should be to guide investors to make decisions that best serve their interests." Effective financial advisors are those who are "guided by an accurate picture of the cognitive and emotional weakness of investors that relate to making investment decisions: their occasionally faulty assessment of their own interests and true wishes, the relevant facts that they tend to ignore, and the limits of their ability to accept advice and to live with the decisions they make." The authors highlight systematic errors of judgment (biases) and errors of preference, which "arise either from mistakes that people make in assigning values to future outcomes or from improper combinations of probabilities and values." For each type of bias or error, the authors introduce a question illustrating it and offer recommendations to financial advisors on how to mitigate it. At the end of the article, Kahneman and Riepe provide financial advisors with a checklist that asks how frequently they perform certain tasks that could help investors avoid investing pitfalls. The paper has five sections: (1) "Introduction," (2) "Errors of Preference," (3) "The Purchase Price as a Reference Point," (4) "Living with the Consequences of Decisions," and (5) "A Checklist for Financial Advisors."

Retirement Saving Adequacy

Lusardi, Annamaria, and Olivia S. Mitchell. "Financial Literacy and Planning: Implications for Retirement Wellbeing." Michigan Retirement Research Center Research Paper No. WP 2005–108 (December 2005): 1–28. *http://papers.ssrn.com/sol3/papers.cfm?abstract_id*=881847 (accessed May 24, 2010).

Abstract: Annamaria Lusardi is an economics professor at Dartmouth College, and Olivia Mitchell is a professor at the University of Pennsylvania specializing in pension research. Based on a brief survey of American households conducted in conjunction with the 2004 Health and Retirement Study, the authors find evidence of widespread financial illiteracy, particularly among women, minorities, and those without a college degree. The survey consisted of three questions about compound interest, inflation, and stock risk. Furthermore, the authors discover a linkage between financial literacy and retirement planning. The financially literate who do plan tend to use formal tools and methods rather than relying on relatives and co-workers for advice. Since planning is related to investment success, wide disparities in household wealth upon retirement are not surprising. Overall, only a minority of households feel "confident" about retirement saving adequacy. The authors recommend financial education programs targeting the least financially sophisticated segments of the population. The paper has four sections: 1) "Approach and Data," 2) "Descriptive Findings," 3) "Multivariate Regression Analysis," and 4) "Implications and Conclusions."

Samwick, Andrew A., and Jonathan Skinner. "How Will 401(k) Pension Plans Affect Retirement Income?" *The American Economic Review* 94, no. 1 (March 2004): 329–43. Available: http://www.dartmouth.edu/~jskinner/documents/SamwickAAHowWill401k.pdf (accessed January 12, 2010).

Abstract: Andrew Samwick and Jonathan Skinner are economics professors at Dartmouth College. Given the shift from defined benefit (DB) to defined contribution (DC) plans over the past two decades, the authors address the issue whether DC plans provide the same level of retirement income. For data they use Surveys of Consumer Finances from 1983 to 2001 and the associated Pension Provider Surveys for 1983 and 1989. The authors' primary finding is that from either of those two years to 1995, the typical 401(k) plan offered roughly equivalent benefits to comparable DB plans. Even more surprisingly, by the end of the decade of the 1990s the typical 401(k) plan offered superior results to all but the most risk-averse consumers. Therefore, the authors conclude that contrary to popular perception, DC plans have improved current workers' retirement security. The paper has six sections: (1) "Introduction," (2) "Modeling the distribution of DB and DC pension benefits," (3) "Data and parameterization," (4) "Empirical results," (5) "Are workers really better off under DC plans?" and (6) "Conclusion."

Skinner, Jonathan. "Are You Sure You're Saving Enough for Retirement?" *Journal of Economic Perspectives* 21, no. 3 (Summer 2007): 59–80. Available by subscription: http://search. ebscohost.com/ (accessed January 5, 2010). Also available: http://www.dartmouth.edu/~jskinner/documents/SkinnerAreyouSure.pdf (accessed January 15, 2010).

Abstract: Jonathan Skinner, an economics professor at Dartmouth College, uses the life-cycle model to examine the question of whether people are saving enough for retirement. The life- cycle model assumes that consumption remains flat over the course of a person's lifetime, as retirees tap into savings accumulated during their careers. Skinner attempts to determine how much nonhousing net worth retired people require to smooth consumption. He provides a table displaying the target nonhousing-wealth-to-income ratio for different ages, according to the life- cycle model, as well as sensitivity analyses for a number of factors, such as savings rates; retirement ages; death ages; consumption declines at retirement, and replacement rates of retirement income, relative to preretirement income, earnings, and consumption growth. One sensitivity analysis shows that housing wealth is a powerful tool for "attenuating the need to accumulate nonhousing wealth for retirement." Another interesting finding is that those who save at high rates during their working lives are accustomed to consuming less and, therefore, do not need as much for retirement. Because they have set aside more, this pattern of saving and consuming less provides them with a "double dividend". Therefore, the author recommends saving incrementally more each year. In a second chart, Skinner shows targets for nonhousing wealth in dollar amounts for various ages and types of households. The author explains that, even if most American households fall short of the targets that the life-cycle model stipulates, they may have lower expenses during retirement, except for health care expenses, and may find they are able to compensate for inadequate savings by economizing. However, Skinner identifies growing out-of-pocket health care costs as a cause for concern. The paper has five sections: (1) "Introduction," (2) "Retirement Saving in a Life-Cycle Model," (3) "How Much Money Do You Really Need to Enjoy Retirement?" (4) "The Real Worry: Growing Out-of-Pocket Health Care Costs," and (5) "Conclusion."

GLOSSARY

Actively managed funds—Funds in which the portfolio manager has discretion over purchases, in contrast to index funds, which mirror a benchmark index. Actively managed funds carry higher fees than index funds.

Affect—Perception of goodness or badness. Affective thinking is based on emotion rather than on rationality.

Agency costs—The costs of delegating investment decisions to a portfolio manager or financial advisor. The adviser's (agent's) interests may not coincide with those of the investor (principal). Therefore, costs are not just monetary.

Alpha—Excess return of a fund, relative to a benchmark index.

Anchor and adjustment heuristic—Starting with an estimate based on a known value, such as past performance, and then making minor adjustments to arrive at a final estimate. For example, annuity investors take into account recent returns, projecting the same return for the next period, without taking into account a long-term investment horizon.

Asset allocation—The strategy of choosing among various asset classes with different risk and return characteristics—for example, equities/stocks, fixed-income securities/bonds, cash equivalents, commodities, and real estate)—in creating a portfolio.

Balanced style of investing—Creating an investment portfolio that produces both capital appreciation and income.

Bayesian statistics—A form of statistical inference in which the statistician uses new evidence to update or revise prior estimates of probabilities (named for British mathematician Thomas Bayes).

Behavioral finance—An emerging field, highlighting observable, systematic, and human departures from rational behavior in investing.

Behavioral portfolio theory—An alternative theory to the widely accepted mean-variance portfolio theory. According to behavioral portfolio theory, which was developed by Hersh Shefrin and Meir Statman of Santa Clara University, portfolios consist of a combination of bonds and lottery tickets, as investors distinguish between investments that offer upside potential and those that offer protection from loss.

Benchmark index—A point of reference for investors and fund managers. For example, the Standard & Poor's 500 Index provides the point of reference for measuring performance of domestic equity fund managers.

Beta—Correlation between a security's returns and market swings. A beta of 1 indicates that a security moves in perfect synchronization with the market. A beta of 1.2 indicates that it is 20 percent more volatile than the market.

Book-to-market ratio—The balance sheet carrying value of a security, relative to its market value. A low book-to-market ratio implies a high valuation.

Buy-and-hold strategy—An investment strategy that favors long-term investments over frequent trading.

Capital asset pricing model (CAPM)—A model used to estimate the expected return of an asset, given that asset's nondiversifiable risk. According to CAPM, developed by financial economist William Sharpe, the expected return is equal to the risk-free rate, plus beta, times the difference between the expected market return and the risk-free rate:

$$E(Ri) = Rf + f3i(E(R_m) - Rf)$$

where:

$E(R_i)$= is the expected return on an asset i,

R_f is the risk-free rate (see glossary definition),

β_i is the asset's beta (see glossary definition), and

$E(R_m)$ is the expected return of the market.

Conjoint analysis—A statistical technique in which consumers make trade-offs among combinations of product features or attributes.

Contrarian investing—Investing in a manner opposed to conventional wisdom or consensus opinion. Underlying the practice of contrarian investing is the assumption that herd behavior leads to mistakenly priced securities.

Defined benefit savings plan—A retirement plan that promises a specified monthly benefit, usually based on a formula that takes into account salary and length of service.

Defined contribution saving plan—A retirement plan based on investment returns from periodic contributions by the employee or employer or both.

Disposition effect—The tendency of investors to sell winning positions and hold onto losing positions.

Efficient market hypothesis (EMH)—The theory that market prices reflect all known information, with the implication that beating the market by identifying undervalued securities is impossible. Economist Eugene Fama developed EMH.

Equity home bias—The tendency to invest in stocks of domestic companies, thereby failing to take advantage of international diversification.

Equity risk premium—Excess return over the risk-free rate, of an individual stock or of the stock market.

Ex-dividend date—Two business dates before the record date for a dividend. For an investor to receive the dividend, the company must have recorded the investor in its books as a shareholder on the record date. Because a trade takes three days to settle, an investor who purchases a stock on or after the ex-dividend date is not eligible to receive the dividend.

Factor model regression—Regression demonstrating the impact of more than one factor on the relationship between the dependent variable (the portfolio's return) and the independent variable (the overall market's return). For example, Eugene Fama and Kenneth French developed a three- factor regression model for portfolio analysis, in which the three factors are beta, exposure to small capitalization stocks, and exposure to high book-to-market value stocks.

Familiarity bias—The tendency to invest in what one knows best from personal experience, such as the stock of one's own company or of companies in the geographical vicinity.

Glamour stock—A high-growth, well-known, trendy stock.

Growth style of investing—An approach to investing that focuses on high-growth stocks, even if they have high price-to-earning ratios. The growth style contrasts with the value style.

Herd behavior—The tendency of investors, like a herd of animals, to follow the group. Such conformity can give rise to bubbles in individual securities and market sectors.

Heuristics—Rules of thumb.

Index funds—Funds that mirror a benchmark index, such as the Standard & Poor's 500, and that charge low fees.

Information advantage or asymmetry—When an individual has special insights into an investment, through knowledge that is not available to others. Trading on such inside information is illegal.

Informational cascades—Deciding how to act from observing others, rather than relying on one's own signals.

Institutional investors—Fiduciary entities established to manage client assets with full investment discretion. Institutional investors include banks and bank trust departments; insurance companies; investment advisors; investment companies (mutual-fund families); and endowments, philanthropic foundations, and public and corporate pension funds.

Intraday price—The price of a security during the trading day, as opposed to the closing price.

Life-cycle model of investing—A model of investing over a lifetime, which assumes that consumption remains flat as retirees tap into savings accumulated during their careers.

Loss aversion—Tendency in investors to have greater sensitivity to losses than to gains of the same size. Loss aversion is an element of prospect theory developed by psychologists Daniel Kahneman and Amos Tversky.

Loss avoidance system—A brain system linked to the avoidance of risk in investing. According to neuroscientists, the loss avoidance system transmits signals via serotonin and norepinephrine.

Mean-variance portfolio theory—Synonymous with "Modern portfolio theory (MPT)" (see glossary entry).

Mental accounting—The process whereby people mentally code, categorize, and frame the outcomes associated with economic decisions. An example is the tendency to invest "new money" and "old money" differently.

Modern portfolio theory (MPT)—A theory of investing developed by economist Harry Markowitz. MPT holds that combining a diversified portfolio, located on the efficient frontier, with the risk-free asset, funded by borrowing, leads to a better return than that achieved on the efficient frontier alone. In other words, the addition of the risk-free asset to the optimal, but risky, portfolio improves the risk-return trade-off. The efficient frontier is the single portfolio that offers the maximum return for a given level of risk. The diversified portfolio eliminates unsystematic risk (risk associated with a specific stock).

Momentum investing—The investment strategy of buying securities with high recent returns and selling those with low recent returns, in the expectation that past trends will continue. This strategy conflicts with the efficient market hypothesis (EMH).

Mutual fund expense ratio—Operating expenses divided by average assets under management. Operating expenses include management fees, distribution and service fees, and other expenses. The expense ratio quantifies the cost of owning a fund.

Mutual fund load fees—Sales charges or commissions that compensate brokers. Investors pay front-end loads up front, upon purchase, and pay back-end loads upon redemption. Front-end and back-end loads are not included in a fund's operating expenses.

Myopic loss aversion—The combination of loss aversion and the tendency, even of long-term investors, to evaluate a portfolio frequently. Shlomo Benartzi and Richard H. Thaler proposed this concept.

Naïve diversification—An approach toward asset allocation in which, given *n* options, investors allocate their assets proportionally among those options, so that each option receives *1/n* of the total.

Narrow framing—Thinking about gambles or investments in isolation, rather than as part of a portfolio with a combination of risks.

Noise trading—Trading on spurious, uninformative signals, such as rumors.

Ponzi scheme—A scheme that involves a swindler who raises money from investors to pay off prior investors. The Ponzi scheme takes its name from Charles Ponzi, who committed a fraud of this type in the early 1900s.

Prescriptive analysis—A type of thinking related to practical advice, which helps people make more rational decisions. Investment advisors offer prescriptive analysis.

Price persistence—Price change of a security over an interval of time, relative to an index (also known as relative strength). Momentum investors highly value price persistence.

Price-to-earning (P/E) ratio—Stock price divided by earnings per share. The P/E ratio measures how expensive a stock is on a normalized basis.

Proprietary traders—Traders who are employees of an investment bank and trade securities on behalf of the firm, rather than on behalf of customers.

Prospect theory—How people maximize value or utility functions in choosing between alternatives that involve risk. Psychologists Daniel Kahneman and Amos Tversky developed prospect theory.

Random-walk theory of investing—A theory associated with economist Burton G. Malkiel, holding that, in a price series for securities, all subsequent price changes represent random departures from previous prices.

Rational choice theory—A theory holding that investors reason before taking action (making an investment), weighing the costs and benefits of that action (investment).

Rational expectations theory—Economists' assumption that people behave (invest) in ways that maximize utility (returns).

Relative optimism—The tendency of investors to favor investing in their home country because they are more optimistic about its performance than about the performance of foreign markets.

Representativeness heuristic—The tendency to see patterns in truly random sequences.

Reputational interactions—Taking into account mutual impact among parties.

Reward approach system—A brain system linked to risk taking in investing. According to neuroscientists, the reward approach system transmits signals via the "pleasure chemical" dopamine.

Risk-free rate—The rate of return on a U.S. Treasury security.

Search problem—The challenge of selecting stocks for purchase from the universe of available stocks.

Self-attribution bias—Ascribing successes to personal abilities and failures to bad luck or to the actions of others.

Sensitivity analysis—In a mathematical model, the impact on outputs of changes in inputs.

Smoothing consumption—A concept proposed by proponents of the life-cycle model of investing, positing that consumption remains flat (is smoothed) as retirees tap into savings accumulated during their careers.

Social learning—Learning from observing others.

Stop-loss orders—An order to sell a security when its price has dropped below a specified threshold.

Survivorship bias—The disappearance of failed companies from performance indexes so that they present misleading results.

Transaction costs—Costs incurred from buying or selling securities, such as brokerage commissions.

Value style of investing—Buying out-of-favor stocks that have low price-to-earnings and priceto-book value ratios and that the investor believes are trading below their intrinsic value.

Wildcard option (for equity mutual funds)—Trading shares at stale prices, an option that is available because some stocks included in a mutual fund portfolio do not trade in the last two hours of each day.

CHAPTER SOURCES

The following chapters have been previously published:

Chapter 1 – This is an edited reformatted and augmented version of a Library of Congress publication, report, *Behavioral Patterns and Pitfalls of U.S. Investors*, dated August 2010.

Chapter 2 – This is an edited reformatted and augmented version of a Library of Congress publication, report *Annotated Bibliography on the Behavioral Characteristics of U.S. Investors*, dated August 2010.

INDEX

A

academic journal articles, vii, 1
access, 49
accounting, 28, 67
adjustment, 65
adults, 33
agencies, 14
anxiety, 58
arbitrage, 37
aspiration, 60
assessment, 62
assets, 11, 28, 33, 49, 67, 68
asymmetric information, 3, 24, 59
asymmetry, 67
attribution, 2, 25, 39, 69
attribution bias, 2, 25, 39, 69
aversion, 8, 13, 25, 32, 42, 43, 52, 67, 68
avoidance, 24, 57, 67
awareness, 58

B

balance sheet, 65
banking, 46
bankruptcy, 9
banks, 49, 67
base, 35, 37, 38, 39, 43, 44, 60
behavioral finance, vii, 1, 2, 4, 9, 14, 18, 23, 24, 25, 28, 32, 36, 38, 42, 45, 61
behaviors, 38, 44
benchmarks, 9, 34, 60
benefits, 33, 46, 63, 69
bias, 7, 9, 29, 34, 45, 60, 62, 66, 67, 70
blame, 9, 29
bonds, 5, 42, 47, 54, 65
brain, 24, 57, 61, 67, 69
brain chemistry, 61
business cycle, 10
buyers, 11, 37

C

capital asset pricing model (CAPM), 27, 34
capital gains, 53
capital markets, 6, 43
case study, 59
cash, 31, 36, 65
cash flow, 36
causal relationship, 54
challenges, vii, 23
chemical, 58, 69
Chicago, viii, 6, 8, 18, 23, 28, 30, 31, 40, 42, 47, 53
classes, 65
clients, 14, 37
cognitive ability, 4, 54
college students, 35
community, vii, 23
compensation, 9, 31

compulsive behavior, 58
conformity, 67
Congress, v, 1, 23
consensus, 66
consulting, 37
consumers, 63, 66
consumption, 4, 6, 32, 41, 63, 67, 69
correlation, 7, 38, 54
cost, 13, 57, 68
covering, 29, 38
crises, 10
customers, 69

D

data analysis, 44
database, 29, 34, 49
decision makers, 20
dependent variable, 66
depression, 58, 61
diffusion, 11, 45, 55
disclosure, 8, 14, 25, 43, 56, 59
disposition, 2, 7, 25, 38, 41, 46, 49
distress, 10, 55
distribution, 50, 63, 68
diversification, 5, 7, 9, 11, 12, 25, 28, 29, 32, 33, 45, 50, 54, 59, 60, 66, 68
dopamine, 58, 61, 69

E

earnings, 13, 26, 40, 47, 51, 64, 69, 70
economic theory, 4, 32, 38
economics, vii, 3, 6, 16, 20, 24, 31, 40, 41, 44, 47, 49, 54, 55, 59, 60, 62, 63
education, viii, 6, 23, 25, 27, 30, 31, 35, 54, 56, 57, 63
efficient market hypothesis (EMH), vii, 23, 40, 47, 68
emotion, 3, 61, 64
employees, 4, 9, 14, 27, 28, 29, 30, 31, 69
employers, 9, 11, 14, 29, 30
empowerment, 30
endowments, 42, 49, 67
England, 61
enrollment, 4, 14, 30, 31, 32, 33
environment, 55
equities, 9, 26, 29, 60, 65
equity, 9, 12, 25, 26, 29, 33, 34, 41, 42, 47, 56, 59, 60, 65, 70
Eugene Fama, viii, 23, 47, 66
euphoria, 10, 58
evidence, vii, 1, 8, 34, 35, 37, 40, 47, 48, 50, 53, 62, 65
exposure, 50, 66

F

families, 49, 67
fear, 4, 6, 41, 53, 58, 61
Federal Research Division, v, vii, 1, 23
financial, 2, 3, 4, 5, 8, 10, 12, 13, 14, 25, 26, 30, 31, 35, 37, 38, 45, 47, 52, 54, 58, 59, 61, 62, 64, 65
financial markets, 2, 4, 38
fluctuations, 41
force, 60
formula, 66
foundations, 2, 49, 67
framing, 32, 43, 52, 68
fraud, 3, 26, 58, 59, 68
funds, 7, 8, 24, 25, 27, 28, 33, 34, 35, 42, 48, 49, 50, 56, 57, 64, 67, 70

G

gender differences, 52
greed, 4, 61
growth, 10, 12, 13, 36, 41, 50, 51, 64, 67
growth rate, 13, 51

H

health, 7, 64
health care, 7, 64
health care costs, 64
historical data, 41
history, 44, 55

housing, 10, 64
human, vii, 2, 4, 20, 38, 50, 61, 65
human psychology, 38
hypothesis, vii, 23, 24, 40, 46, 47, 48, 61, 66, 68

I

illiteracy, 4, 5, 25, 54, 62
illusion, 39
income, 4, 10, 25, 50, 52, 63, 64, 65
independent variable, 66
individuals, vii, 1, 4, 20, 30, 32, 35, 42, 45
industry, 46
inertia, 4, 31, 32
inflation, 5, 54, 62
institutions, 48
intelligence, 20
interest rates, 5, 54
intrinsic value, 11, 13, 14, 44, 51, 70
investment, vii, 2, 3, 4, 6, 7, 8, 9, 10, 12, 14, 25, 29, 31, 35, 36, 43, 44, 46, 49, 50, 51, 52, 56, 58, 61, 62, 63, 64, 65, 66, 67, 68, 69
investment bank, 14, 51, 69
investments, 8, 12, 13, 14, 25, 29, 33, 35, 40, 43, 45, 46, 59, 65, 68
investor behavior, vii, viii, 1, 23, 24, 30, 44, 46
investors, vii, 1, 2, 3, 4, 6, 7, 8, 9, 10, 11, 12, 13, 14, 23, 25, 26, 27, 28, 31, 32, 33, 34, 35, 36, 37, 38, 39, 40, 41, 42, 43, 45, 46, 47, 48, 49, 51, 52, 53, 56, 57, 58, 59, 60, 61, 62, 65, 66, 67, 68, 69
Ireland, 49
isolation, 68
issues, 60

J

justification, 60

L

lack of confidence, 33
lead, 1, 2, 10, 11, 14, 35, 41
learning, 69
lifetime, 4, 6, 32, 64, 67
light, 2, 10, 24, 55
liquidity, 48
literacy, 5, 8, 13, 35, 52, 54, 62
loyalty, 9, 29

M

magical thinking, 4, 10, 61
management, 8, 14, 31, 49, 51, 68
mania, 7, 10, 58
marketing, 33, 56
media, 13, 51
median, 56
medical, 4, 57, 61
mental illness, 58
metaphor, 10
methodology, 34
minorities, 5, 62
models, 2, 24, 36, 38
modern portfolio theory (MPT), 27
momentum, 7, 10, 35, 40, 44, 47, 61
monopoly, 12
Montana, 45
multiples, 47
myopia, 8

N

neglect, 4
Netherlands, 5
neuroscience, 24, 57
neurotransmitter, 61
neutral, 52
Nobel Prize, 2, 12, 61
norepinephrine, 58, 67

O

opportunities, 28
opt out, 14, 33
optimism, 2, 9, 10, 25, 27, 55, 60, 69
overweight, 57
ownership, 9, 29

P

participants, 4, 6, 27, 29, 30, 31, 43, 52
pastures, 48
penalties, 3, 59
pension plans, 43
performers, 8
pleasure, 58, 69
policy, 31
poor performance, 35
population, 6, 54, 63
portfolio, 8, 9, 10, 12, 25, 26, 27, 32, 34, 35, 37, 43, 45, 46, 47, 49, 50, 55, 59, 64, 65, 66, 67, 68, 70
poverty, 60
price changes, 47, 69
principles, 12
professionals, vii, 14, 51, 61
profitability, 50
project, 13
prospect theory, 2, 24, 32, 41, 42, 46, 67, 69
protection, 60, 65
psychologist, 2, 24
psychology, vii, 2, 3, 14, 24, 61
public policy, 31, 55

R

rate of return, 69
rational expectations, vii, 1, 2, 14, 23
rationality, 4, 11, 20, 28, 32, 38, 44, 64
real estate, 65
recommendations, 62
Regional Bell Operating Companies, 45
Regional Bell Operating Companies (RBOCs), 45
regression, 34, 49, 66
regression model, 66
regulations, 29
relatives, 6, 63
replacement rate, 64
representativeness, 36, 40
representativeness heuristic, 40
requirements, 30
researchers, 35
resistance, 30
resources, 4, 32
response, 39
restrictions, 36
retail, 25, 37, 49, 52
retirement, 4, 6, 9, 11, 14, 25, 26, 27, 28, 31, 32, 54, 62, 63, 66
retirement age, 64
rewards, 3, 59
risk, 1, 2, 5, 9, 13, 24, 25, 27, 32, 34, 41, 42, 43, 47, 48, 49, 50, 52, 53, 54, 57, 58, 59, 60, 62, 63, 65, 66, 67, 68, 69
risk aversion, 2, 13, 24, 52
risk factors, 49, 58
risks, 3, 29, 36, 41, 59, 68
rules, 27, 28

S

savings, 6, 9, 27, 28, 29, 30, 31, 32, 64, 66, 67, 69
savings rate, 28, 30, 64
school, vii, 8, 10, 23, 42, 44
scope, viii, 23
securities, viii, 10, 23, 35, 36, 47, 65, 66, 67, 68, 69, 70
security, 9, 50, 63, 65, 67, 69, 70
self-control, 4, 32, 50
self-discipline, 58
self-interest, vii, 1, 14, 23
sensitivity, 43, 64, 67
serotonin, 58, 67
services, 8, 31, 35
shape, 28
signals, 11, 43, 58, 67, 68, 69
signs, 58

simulation, 33
simulations, 42
social learning, 43
social sciences, 24
sociology, vii, 2, 24
solution, 33, 59
specialists, 9, 12
specialization, 46
speculation, 10, 55, 61
Spring, 56
staff members, 35
standard of living, 6
state, 9, 45
states, 9, 45
statistical inference, 65
statistics, 34, 65
stock markets, 47
stock price, vii, 11, 23, 40, 44, 47
structure, 4, 32, 57
style, 13, 37, 49, 50, 51, 65, 67, 70
Styles, 50
subscribers, 27
Sun, 26
susceptibility, 3
synchronization, 65

T

target, 54, 57, 64
taxes, 53
technologies, 14
technology, 13, 51, 55
telephone, 7, 39
time series, 41
tracks, 37
trade, 27, 32, 38, 39, 66, 68, 69, 70
trade-off, 32, 66, 68
transaction costs, 8, 34, 35
trial, 43
triggers, 3

U

U.S. Treasury, 69
United Kingdom, (UK) 9, 17, 19, 32, 60
United States, 53, 61
universe, 37, 56, 69
University of California at Los Angeles (UCLA), 27
University of Chicago, viii, 23, 47

V

valuation, 47, 65
variations, 33
volatility, 11, 50
vulnerability, 60

W

Washington, 48
weakness, 62
wealth, 2, 6, 32, 41, 63, 64
web, 52, 56, 57, 58
workers, 63
workplace, 31

Y

Yale University, 41, 55
yield, 25